HOLOGRAM OF THE SOUL

By Anne Spieker

Contents

ACKNOWLEDGEMENTS

I would like to thank my dear friend Joe, who has been with me since 1994, watching the ebb and flow of an outwardly strong individual that was emotionally guided and held up by a weak navigational system. Joe always believed that I was the greatest and sweetest person he ever knew, even if I didn't believe those sentiments myself. He and I may not agree on how we approach every aspect of life, but one thing we whole heartedly agree upon is that no one should ever steal your soul.

I also want to thank my family for their love and support through every twist, turn, move, mate, trauma, and challenge I've encountered in my life. They are the strongest people I know, Joe included. They say, "Surround yourself with strong people," and, well, I was blessed with amazing diversity and strength right in my own family.

Even when you think you are alone in the world, you aren't, because within you is a soul that is your closest and best friend of all. When you understand the chemistry within your own soul you'll never be alone again.

PREFACE

Hologram of the Soul came about because I wanted to share with others the secrets to self-confidence, self-love, and prolonged personal happiness. For a long time, I allowed outside opinions to direct my emotional intelligence and personal happiness. I realized that I had to manage my thoughts and, my emotional intelligence and feelings in order to be on a path of self-love, continued calmness, and self-assuredness. I didn't need anyone's approval to be happy or to live my life the way it was meant to be lived. Before the realization—that I can have my own thoughts and emotions—I would teeter on the brink of self-doubt and fear of never being "enough," or worthy of anything good. I was navigating life with an emotional intelligence that was hindering me, not guiding me. If our emotional foundation is one that is rickety, broken, or constructed out of only other people's thoughts, we will retreat to a place of isolation, self-abuse, and deprivation in efforts to conform to what someone else made us believe that we are. The people in your life who are suffering emotionally will find victims to project their unhealthy emotional selves onto, whether they do so intentionally or not. That's just how it works. But what if your reception of these negative influences happened when you were unknowing, didn't understand, and didn't suspect that such a thing could happen?

In this book, I make it my purpose to let you know that it does happen. Imagine being a highly intelligent, feeling, and sensitive child—or adult—absorbing all that is presented, being directed by what other's feel, say, or do to you. Imagine that what you were fed at that time isn't the truth at all. The information you were taking in wasn't your own set of values or beliefs or intelligence at all. It's like being fed bad intelligence over and over and over. When I would intellectually and emotionally repeat the negative sentiments that others had or said about me, I became depressed and conflicted internally. Now, when I listen to my own thoughts, emotions, and feelings about myself, I present a strong, vibrant, happy smile on my face, showing true happiness with myself. I finally figured out I was tapping into untruths and feelings that were not mine at all. I was hosting others' emotional intelligence. There was such a sense of urgency to understand why I felt the way I did, that once I figured it out, I had to share it with everyone. If I can help one person on their journey to personal happiness, it is all worth it.

Chapter 1

Absorption in that Instant

The journey of *Hologram of the Soul* begins at the place where our soul begins to fill with the emotional intellect we host and use to become the person we know we are, for the rest of our lives: our foundational set of values, self-awareness, esteem, and understanding. There are life-moments in our formative years (0-18 years of age) from which we absorb the emotional intelligence of those around us and from our environmental influences. Whether you are an only child, baby of the family, or the oldest or middle child, you are influenced and shaped by all the humans in your immediate circle of influence and absorb their goodness, sadness, baggage, feelings, emotions, encounters, words, efficiencies, inefficiencies and—oddly enough—their projections. All of this, along with their support, nurturing, love, or lack of love, fuels the soul, creating a lifelong guidance system that we tap into and use each day for strength.

This book isn't about learning how to balance a checkbook, clean your bedroom, or do your homework; those are all good lessons, and hopefully you've picked them up along the way, but what I am referring to is how to understand the emotional intelligence absorbed very early in life, before our receptors work intelligently. The personal work can begin as soon as you recognize that you are living an emotionally unhealthy and unhappy life. Living a quality, emotionally intelligent life takes some personal internal work. The outcome of this personal work, however, is a state of happiness for the remainder of your life, resulting in a beautiful hologram!

The life you lead today is a compilation of generational improvements and mishaps, which contribute to whether yours is a lifetime afflicted with unresolved emotional baggage, or a lifetime of phenomenal happiness, health, and success. Who you are today isn't about *blaming* the generation that raised you or the environmental factors that shaped you, or any neglect, hurt, shame, or abuse you encountered as a non-participatory, unsuspecting child. It's about breaking away from the influence of the emotional intelligence you inherited (or absorbed) and becoming who you were meant to be.

Who you are today was derived from the emotional intelligence gleaned from every person and activity you encountered during the formative years of your life. It was essentially by osmosis. Regardless of your place in life—because you can't pick the city you were born in, your family of origin, family members (or their ideations), schools, teachers, mentors or extracurricular activities—you can choose what emotions serve you and which do not. Learning about your emotional intelligence and how it is acquired will heal emotional wounds so you can become the beautiful, healthy, and vibrant human you were meant to be, one that shines love and light to everyone in your home, workplace, and everywhere you go.

As an empath and trained certified master life coach, I've been so fortunate to have had many discussions with those suffering emotionally from words, events, feelings—a whole neurology—that evolved from their total life experience from their first 18 years of life. Having never addressed their core concerns, a lot of people report to feeling less than ideal in terms of their personal happiness, awareness, and growth. Living life without ever confronting and working through the emotional traumas of the formative years means living a sadder life than warranted. It's your job to ask yourself, *why do I feel the way I do?* It's like carrying around everyone else's emotions until you realize you can shed them and become who YOU are, as opposed to who you became through absorption. Even more unfortunately, not only did my clients feel shameful and sad, but they then cast those negative feelings and emotions onto their children, spouses, and, eventually, their coworkers, throughout their lives. It's the cycle of emotional intelligence that is derived from others and subsequently projected onto others when, in reality, it isn't even YOU!

Giving thought to and taking care of our souls—which host all the absorbed emotions throughout our life—will reflect on our face and in how we live our lives. While no one promised us roses and sugar cookies, life has beautiful things that are waiting for us all when we clean up our soul reservoir. It's not so bad digging and finding the things that keep us down, unhappy, or angry. It's good, clean work.

In the very beginning, when we are impressionable and vulnerable, our souls inhale and absorb positive and negative emotions directly from our environment, aiding in either healthy or unhealthy personal self-esteem and in productive or unproductive behaviors. We cannot choose the geographical location or the familial environment into which we are born. Some get the short end of the stick, while others get the silver platter. It is what it is, but it doesn't need to stay that way forever! Our parents and other adult influencers came to the party with baggage, learned behaviors, strengths, and weaknesses from their childhoods as well. Parents and adults do their best to manage their own emotional reservoir and to create a new one for their child, but if the parent or influencer never confronts and addresses their own core issues, they'll likely infuse those issues, and their attached emotions, onto an unsuspecting child or person.

The interesting part is, if your parents—or their parents, or *their* parents—were shorted or stunted emotionally, you will be shorted and stunted also. It is up to you to find those "hurts" and heal them. It is your duty, right, and privilege to be healthy and to impart healthiness unto others around you.

We've all heard the saying, "the acorn doesn't fall far from the tree." However, the acorn must make its way farther from the tree in order for the emotional intelligence to develop and flourish in a healthy, happy, productive way. I believe you must understand how a healthy or unhealthy emotionally healthy soul begins.

Many things in our life can and will happen "in an instant." The weather can change in an instant (especially if you live in the Upper Midwest.) You can be in the middle of a gorgeous sunny day, and, suddenly, in a flash, big drops of rain fall on your head like June bugs hitting a window.

Like understanding that weather can turn, we must understand that things happen to us—changing our emotional state and feelings of self-worth—*in an instant*. The soul reservoir, from which our self-worth and self-esteem guidance system derives its power, can and will be changed in an instant as a child. It can happen at home, at school, in some of the most familiar or unfamiliar settings. Later in this book, I'll address simple secrets to help you diffuse unwanted energy that might arrive at your soul's door as an adult, and keep that uninvited energy at bay, so that it doesn't infuse and taint your soul chemistry. But when you are a child, it can happen when you can't or don't suspect or deserve it.

To establish ongoing happiness, you must know which messages are good, real, truthful, and coming from a reliable, healthy source. You must be able to choose which feelings and emotions to take in, keep, store and develop within your self-esteem, and which messages must be ignored. This is paramount in the learning curve of ongoing life happiness.

We hear people talk about "the tapes," the negative messaging that fills the brain and exists in a repeating loop. We are not born with negative emotions that cause us to self-abuse, to dislike, or lean into obsession or more dysfunction. We inherit and absorb good and bad feelings along the way, and most of us aren't aware that this transmission is taking place. As an adult, before you can create a new life for yourself, and end the obnoxious cycle, you must learn about your emotional wellbeing, who you have become, and why. The saying goes, "Happiness is an inside job," and it's true! We'll dig, grow, and you'll find that pure joy and happiness that will follow all the days of your life, when you ask the difficult questions. *Why do I feel this way?*

The incredible forces of an "instant" are strong and understanding when that *instant* occurs is key to personal happiness and emotional stability. At that instant you have to consider what path this chemistry will take if at all. Whether you are absorbing or deflecting, it is an ongoing battle—and duty—to impart and take in healthy emotional energy. We all need tools to discern what emotions are healthy in order to make a home in our soul reservoir. Mastering the ability to discern the emotional energy underlying the words and actions encountered daily as a child, adolescent, and young adult, leads to an emotional health for sustaining life-long happiness. We all blame the generations before ours, but in reality, most of the people who came before us were good people with lousy soul chemistry inherited when they weren't suspecting it. To be aware of your own soul chemistry means changing how you feel and changing the world!

In an instant, you can help free someone cleanse themselves and be free from their emotional struggles by allowing them to share their experiences with you. Recognizing emotions behind your own (or someone else's) state of being is abundantly helpful throughout personal soul life work. Not taking on the emotions or troubles of those around us, while being fully aware and accountable for our own, is critical to our—and the next generation's—positive emotional health.

For those who love history, let's think about *an instant*. The 1940s were uncertain times for America's positioning in the world order. Consider the concept of *an instant* in terms of the landing at Normandy or the detonation of the atomic bomb. Those instants shaped the future for Americans, and if anything in those instants went even slightly differently, the future could have been dramatically different. Emotions of those who witnessed and survived these instants were forever laced with the fear and horror of what humans can do to one another. The experience altered their mental states and therefore those of their children, forever. At the same time, American citizens engaged in jubilant celebrations because the conflict was over. How fascinating to understand that at that moment, the impact was more significant than anyone could imagine then, or now.

Why is "in an instant" so important? I have devoted an entire chapter to the concept because split-second decisions can determine what will follow in your life. Things you say about or to another human can alter their lives forever. A thought, an outcome, a future, an action, a decision, a commitment, a vow, a shift, a glance, an acceptance, a denial, a withdrawal, a rejection, and a nod are all split-second instants that impact life.

When an external message or event infiltrates and infuses your psyche and soul, you have a decision to make, in that instant. Do we let what we are experiencing (feeling, hearing, seeing, or receiving) affect us now, for a while, or forever? What is the source of this feeling or thought process? How does this make us feel? Should we compartmentalize, keep, or destroy the information or emotional message? Our hologram (the effect and aura of our faces) begins to take shape because of all those decision-making instances. Our face is the Hologram of our Soul.

Childhood, when receptors and detectors are not yet awake or functional, is often a challenging time in a person's life. The most positive or negative hologram imprints take place before we reach 18, when most of us have little control and cannot stop the process. As adults, becoming aware of the concept of "in an instant" helps us learn to avoid projecting our baggage, inefficiencies, and inadequacies onto children, spouses, and colleagues. The earlier we develop this skill, and teach it to our children, the sooner our soul (and the souls of those we interact with) can become healthier, calmer, and cleansed.

In an instant, a woman can change from being fertile to hosting a living being within her womb. The only knowledge it is happening belongs to the energy world, as even the woman herself is not aware *in that instant* that she has started a life. In a nanosecond, a life begins, the baby's biological gender is programmed and determined. In another instant, a woman can go from being pregnant to not being pregnant by her own choice; the father may never even know she had conceived. In that instant, lives and destinies are changed forever; lives can be created or destroyed. Likewise, our souls can be scribed a new message that will either live forever or be rejected in terms of our emotional wellbeing. In an instant we can believe something about our self because someone else gave us the message.

In an instant, a single spoken or unspoken word can harm another human's self-esteem and outlook on prejudices or loyalties. Good, bad, or mediocre relationships can morph, become stunted, or mesh based on a few chosen adjectives. In that same instant, that once-close relationship will never be the same because someone said something without thinking, or their immaturity surfaced and scarred someone for life. We've all

11

been in toxic, harmful relationships; clearly, had we slowed down enough for our healthy soul's reservoir to assess the situation correctly, the outcome could have been different.

☼

I was little, my grandpa was calling me names, as he liked to do, and I sounded off, "Well, you look like an anteater!" By the look on his face, you'd have thought I had said something terrible about his mother. For a week, he acted as if I were invisible. He took what I'd said as disrespect, while I only meant to let him know that words hurt, and that I could fight back if I had to! Even words from kids on a playground can alter our self-esteem and the way we view others as we socialize and age. Racism, prejudice, acceptance, love, and loyalties are shaped in nanoseconds. Media regurgitates information to steer your thinking and emotions in an instant. Teachers, doctors, family members, friends—even complete strangers—can scar you for life because their emotional reservoirs are tainted so negatively that they inflict their impurities onto you. Split-second decisions, even from the most unsuspecting person, can alter your destiny forever until you realize your destiny is in your hands and soul.

☼

It was just another day in fourth grade when Sister Rose Catherine decided that she would weigh three young girls in the class. I was a taller, broader gal, while my friend, Sue, was a smaller, stout, well-fed Italian gal. The third girl was a robust, buxom African American. Sister Rose Catherine (who was as skinny as a rail) weighed us, placing the results next to our names on the blackboard. That experience crushed a part of me. To this day, I cannot step on a scale in front of the doctor. At every appointment, I go through a cycle of emotions, movements, and excuses why I cannot be weighed, followed by tears of complete and utter fear and hyper-justification for the numbers on the scale. It is an emotional breakdown I undergo in front of others because Sister Rose Catherine decided in an instant, within an innocent fourth-grade class, to deflect a prejudice of hers onto us. In that instant, Sister Rose Catherine shamed me for being who I was, which altered my perception of myself and how I looked at myself for an awfully long time. That is one small example. We all have our own moments, and we often have *many*.

☼

That, my friend, is the basis for this book: to reveal the importance of keeping adverse circumstances or influences from altering who you will become or how you will

12

feel about yourself. Others' actions can profoundly affect your soul, and if you do not learn how to reject those actions, words, and abuse, they may leave an everlasting disfigurement on your hologram. This book will help you learn to tend to your soul (*soul-tending*) in a positive and perpetual manner because without it, you will continue to carry the baggage of someone else with you.

While we're all affected by world-changing events like 9/11 or Hiroshima, simple everyday occurrences can alter your soul too. If, in an instant, you choose not to address what is happening inside of you—perhaps to spare someone's feelings or due to fear of confrontation—your soul becomes altered. Those instants can reflect positively on your soul the second you detect their occurrence *and wave them off*. Allowing them in or waving them off is the act of soul-tending; it's not about being self-consumed, it is about being *self-aware,* which is necessary for long-term happiness.

Humans function in a world with billions of other people, *and their billions of inherited or environmentally infused emotions.* I can feel the vibrations of humans and the energy emitted from the mass of emotions within them. Being wired this way was not something I asked for and was not "given" at birth. It was something that, over time, I became aware of and understood that I was receiving. This happens for me with animals also, and nothing can stop the vibrational chemical outflow of emotions I receive when I am with another living, breathing entity.

As you progress through this book, you'll learn that shaping your soul and your hologram comes from inputting and storing the correct chemistry and ridding yourself of the incorrect or harmful chemistry you've acquired. You must be able to detect incoming messages, remembering that in an instant, if you use other's unhealthy messages or emotions as a guidance system, life can take on a new direction. Knowing who you are and what you want and learning what you can control versus what you cannot are all vital tools in reaching everlasting joy and happiness.

How do you know when you are receiving information that will have a long-term harmful effect on you? Consider the brain as a sponge full of millions of tiny reservoirs, waiting to be filled with "informational chemistry." You cannot stop these craters from filling, but you *do have a choice* as to what you fill these craters with. I call that "conscious allowance." Position yourself well and accept informational chemistry that is healthy and will serve you.

Knowing whether the incoming information chemistry is harmful is determined by how your soul reacts to the information chemistry, positively or negatively. If you are not listening or feeling, you will "hear" and feel nothing. If you *are* listening and feeling, you will feel something in your soul, which I call the "gut soul reactor." At that impeding time, you have every right to make a solid decision regarding the information. *Is this something useful? Will it help me now or in the long-term?* In efforts to make a decision like this you have to be in tune with that gut soul reaction.

Many people were raised or put into an environment of some abuse, neglect, or dysfunction, which might manifest in mental, emotional, and/or physical harm. The information obtained through the filter of an emotional or physical abuser is jumbled, disjointed, and incongruent, and is projected as such. We know when we feel something icky and we know it doesn't feel right or good. When we are too young to understand the information being deflected at us, we may have a more difficult time later figuring out what is real and what is not. This happens because we are too young, in that instant, to disseminate whether what we are being shown, told, or given, is *the truth*. We are changed forever by the information chemistry we are given and, in most instances, unable to hit the reject button. We believe adults and look at them as all knowing! Even as a tiny baby we can FEEL the chemistries of our parents and start to depend on what we are absorbing around us. There are tons of studies that show that babies are emotionally shaped before their birth. Already, the sponge-like craters are absorbing and filling with polluted, untrue, or loving chemistry. That chemistry we carry and host can be diluted and eventually changed, but it takes work. Once we make the decision to change our soul chemistry, we will lead and live a happier healthier life.

If parents are emotionally unhealthy, they impart unhealthy emotions to their children. A parent calling their child an idiot is likely having a difficult time feeling good about themselves; they're calling *themselves* an idiot, but their child is receiving, hosting and feeling their emotional intellect.

Being so young, it is almost impossible to process those words as an adult might. "Does my father *really mean* what he says? Am I truly an idiot?" So, the child's information reservoir fills with that polluted information. As we mature and grow to feel inadequate or emotional about different things, often the origin rests in something we took in before we had the ability to deflect unhealthy emotional intelligence.

The untruths only stay with us if we do not prove them wrong or dilute them with the truth, and by doing so change our soul's reservoir chemistry. Otherwise, our reservoir becomes "stinky"—and we don't need "stinky" in our lives! We did not put it there, and we do not deserve to host it throughout our entire lives.

Having read this far, I'm positive you understand the direction this book is taking.

In an *instant*, life as we know it can change for the better, or for the worse. It can happen in childhood, adolescence, young adulthood, or even as an adult. Life can change in an instant either by accepting unwanted chemistry or by life throwing a huge curveball at a time we least expect it.

It seemed as if the baby was alive one minute and gone the next. In a single instant, I had to say hello and goodbye. I remember thinking to myself, "How could this be? She isn't going to be here for me to love. After all this time, she just dies?" I did not get it and I certainly did not understand what happened or why. But there was more than one death that day. **I died right alongside her.** Metaphorically, because the life I was going to have and the role I would fulfill existed less than a second, and in an instant, she was only a memory. No time to redesign the plan, no time to start over. It was just...*over*. It hit me like a ton of bricks. *"You there, your baby is gone, deal with it!"* It was lights out, for sure, because no one can prepare you for something as sudden and devastating as this unbelievable incident. It's just impossible.

In memory of my daughter, Melina Corinne Severo, May 18, 2001.

It was at that point that the most unimaginable climb back up began—days, months, and years of the most mind-blowing experience ever: the grieving process. It was such a difficult process to endure and changed my hologram forever, in that instant.

I am positive that things just as difficult as what I lived through in that story have happened to you, and have lived inside of you for a long time. Now it is the time to ask yourself the tough questions.

Chapter 2

The Truth Be Told

This chapter may be difficult to embrace, though the concept of truth is a fascinating philosophical subject to address. For many of us, truth has become convoluted or unrecognizable. We have become a nation of "exceptional deceptionals," knowing that truth can be subjective based on a person's experiences, knowledge, and perception. What is the truth? Is it what someone tells you? Is truth something you read? Is truth something you hear? My truth comes from what my gut tells me, based on knowing of *what I host in my soul reservoir emotional chemistry.*

Too often, we believe that what we see and hear is the absolute truth, when, in reality, what we perceive from that truth could be furthest from the original truth. Behind every message is a thought, and unless we are in the brain of the person thinking the thought, it is impossible to know the "truth" they speak of. By the time we hear it, their truth might have been transposed and convoluted a hundred times over. When do we know, without a doubt, that we are receiving the truth?

Personal happiness and creating a strong Hologram of the Soul begins with being honest with oneself. Somewhere along the line, after years of a trafficked inundation of emotional energy from others, we lose the ability to connect to reality and distinguish our own truth from untruth. We then continue our lives, slogging through emotions to keep moving forward. We dangle, dabble, try and take steps without stopping to access where we are emotionally; what we believe about ourselves *might not be the truth.*

Differentiating between fact, fiction, and interpretation is at the heart of this book, *Hologram of the Soul*. Our reality is based on what we've absorbed along the way. That could be days, years, or quarter-centuries of energy and information. Once we understand that we have an emotional reservoir, we can and should choose the energy,

16

information, emotional and mental traffic, and chemistry we want to allow into emotional dispatch (our psyche) and into our soul. We become so adept at bobbing, weaving, contorting, adapting, adhering, and ducking, that the neurons driving our receptors and gut-chemistry fill up with external chemistry instead of what we *should know* as our absolute personal truth or value system. I am familiar with the power of emotional chemistries released from others; they have affected my self-beliefs in my adult life, as well as my decision-making abilities. As a kid attending a sporting event, I heard a man behind me use the word "Amazon" referring to my stature. It was such a negative interpretation of my size and beauty. I was 5 feet 10 inches tall (and stunning!), but I was well into my fifties before I believed in my heart and SOUL that I was beautiful, inside and out. Even understanding that outward beauty is subjective, it is still detrimental to dislike how you look. Another time, I heard a man say, "You know how much you have to feed them to grow them that big?" Had I not been so sensitive and unaware back then, I'd have kicked his ass from here to the moon! In that era, most women were short and petite. Not me, but there wasn't anything I could do about it.

This is a reminder that what people spew and exhaust as a projection of their own low self-worth and their own belief system can scar someone else *for life*.

Siblings can experience different childhoods despite being raised and nurtured under one roof. The baby of one family may not even realize what the eldest child has been though, and vice-versa. Your soul reservoir may be healthy or unhealthy, despite your place in the family, and it is based on truths given to you by family members, and by complete strangers. Only you can know where you stand and how you feel about yourself right now. Are you happy with yourself? Do you like yourself in every way? If not, it's time to ask the tough questions. *What is my truth about myself today?*

As you formulate the truth about who you are and whether you like yourself, you may find that decision-making has been difficult. How do you know that your decisions are sound? Most people find it hard to manage for too long with important life decisions that go completely against who they are and what they stand for. Deep down, there is a mechanism that won't allow them to be unhappy forever. We must adhere to our own personal truths to make sound decisions, and our souls provide the guidance system for our ultimate happiness. If you do make a decision that goes against the fiber of your being (your own personal truth), your soul will let you know. Too often, we refuse to listen to that small inside voice (or soul's agitation) because it's telling us something we may not want to hear, much less *agree with*. If we do nothing about it, we'll be forever unhappy until we accept the truth *or change what we believe to be true*. Anthony Robbins said, "If you can't, then you must." You must decide to correct how you feel and restructure your hologram by cleansing the soul reservoir of those negative inherited truths while keeping the helpful positive ones intact.

Life changes can begin the instant you decide to be honest with yourself, rid your reservoir of negative emotions, and disallow any more external unhealthy emotional traffic to get at you and dilute your own truth. Don't let others' truths take over how you live your life!

When do we receive the absolute truth? The answer is: when we get it ourselves. Watch a new mother talking to her newborn baby. That infant's fresh emotional dispatch is hosting all sorts of words, feelings, and emotions the mother is projecting. "You look just like grandpa," "You are going to be a basketball player, you are so tall," and "I can tell that your personality is just like your dad's." This child is being told the truth as measured through the mother's references, her soul diagram, and where she is at in this stage in her life. This new mother may be a complete hot mess! But she flagrantly tosses information to her child. Before the baby can utter a single word, he or she is absorbing many external untruths from sources that have never questioned their feelings, beliefs, or values, who have also had their views scribed for them by others. We must take a deep dive inside, culling through our soul reservoir, tossing out the negative emotional intelligences that serve us poorly.

No one has the right to pre-determine your soul diagram before you can imprint it yourself, yet babies can hear you argue with your spouse and can taste your stress cortisol. New babies should be fed streams of music and sounds that mimic love, calmness, and acceptance. Still, typically, all we hear from the moment of birth is noise and words from older humans with their own views of life, which then, through no fault of our infant selves, become *our new view*, too. No wonder we are a nation of deception artists! Born with a clean slate, but soon after we are outside the womb we begin absorbing opinions and values based on someone else's soul diagram (or the size of their pocketbook.) Exposure to "soul pollutants" is the fundamental reason we struggle with our own happiness, never having the chance to form our own belief systems because *others have formed it for us*. The lucky few receive good information, while the unlucky do not. Because we can't pick where we are born or who we are born to, what information we are presented with as small children is a crapshoot.

Fortunately, we don't stay young for long. We take shape as little humans, testing the waters because something internally screams, "Get out of my way, I want to be ME!" As we become more cognitive, we learn to deflect as much of the bombarding information as we can, saving our soul from being shredded by the deluge of incoming nonsense or conflicting truths. Who needs all that noise? Still, we are unsuspecting

18

novices, often not even cognizant that we *have* a soul, and we are left defend ourselves without the proper training. This can prove overwhelming at times, regardless of age. We need role models who prepare us for what is out there, teaching us to be wary of the incoming emotional traffic, and considering that much of what we echo may not be true. Likewise, we create traffic and noise of our own, and should realize that what we say can and will be stored on someone else's soul diagram. Someone else might be affected by your unfounded or ungrounded truth.

Truth be told, "truth" depends on being aware that you are receiving and sending soul information; what you take in is, ultimately, what you will send out. Both factor into your overall happiness but, remember, what you are sending out is critical to the shaping of other souls, and the universe. Are you aware that you are part of that universal transaction? You have an obligation to take ownership of your happiness and to help shape other lives on this planet.

Allow me to share my definition of "the soul" and tell you why this book's title contains that word. While I've enjoyed some great reviews on that title (it tends to spark interest), one person became a bit uptight with my use of "soul." As an atheist, he felt that the word denotes a sort of *spiritual* choice. I explained that I see the soul as a home for feelings and emotions. My explanation seemed to ease his agitation, but he wasn't used to addressing such things. Many people aren't. This man had experienced some serious trauma in his life, which I knew informed his discomfort. He inherited his feelings, doesn't know about soul-tending, and lives a life burdened by emotional baggage. Reminder: the sooner we learn to soul-tender, the sooner we can be fully happy.

Soul: Inside of me, there is a place where all my emotions reside, flourish, or fester. My soul is fueled by my thoughts. Those thoughts come from what I allow into the funnel, and how I filter and stream them on their voyage to their final resting place: the soul reservoir. Ultimately, my thoughts create my soul diagram and my hologram. Left unattended or unexpressed, the soul will fester and cause illness, unhappiness, anger, depression, and expressive incongruences. The hologram of your soul—your face—is determined by the health of your soul and whether you have tended to it along life's way.

The soul is the hub, the server, the kitchen, the corporate headquarters, the nucleus, the drop-zone, the cockpit, command central, square one, the core, the drive shaft, the furnace, the engine, and the main circuit breaker. We spend time, money, and energy tending to everything we own, believe in, want, have, or hope to have, but too often we spend little time tending to the *one place* that drives sustainable happiness. You're probably familiar with the saying, "If Mamma ain't happy, no one is happy." Consider my paraphrase: If your soul ain't happy, you won't be! Since the soul is the fire that illuminates your face, it's up to you to ensure that it burns pure and unpolluted during life's journey.

My goal is to help you get in touch with that fire, burn clean fuel, and experience a calm and happy journey, dependent upon walking in unity with what you know to be true. Since soul-tending determines the condition of your soul, you'll reap what you sow. I want you to reap a "full harvest." For *that*, my friend, is what you and I deserve!

I've found a definition for "truth" that I feel is most applicable to my teaching:

The **truth** *depends on, or is only arrived at by, a legitimate deduction from all the facts which are truly material. – Coleridge*

Another way to express this:
Personal truth is a compilation of feelings, thoughts, ingestion, digestion, expulsion, and retainment of information based on exposure, absorption, receptiveness, and understanding.

Truth is subjective and perceptible. Two people can watch the exact same thing or listen to the exact same person speaking and, yet, each person will leave with a different imprint. Consider a crime or accident scene. There will be 30 eyewitnesses, yet no two accounts of the incident will be the same. Their first-hand truth was based on their interpretation of what they saw, and is essentially predicated on their soul diagram, from years of absorption, tending, or lack thereof.

Since our brain interprets information based on our reservoir of everything we have learned through every channel, truth is infinite and finite simultaneously. One person could believe what they saw or heard while another could reject it based on their knowledge or set of circumstances. That is the beauty of truth: it is up to you to determine what is real and truthful *for you*.

Once you have processed *your* truth from something you heard or read, you put your personal mark on it and spew it back to the world, like the pass-the-secret game. One person starts a secret, and it travels through everyone in the room until the last person says what they were told. I haven't been in a room yet where the secret ended precisely as it when it began!

Truth is in the eye of the beholder, in the ear of the beholder, in the touch of the beholder, in the taste of the beholder, and in the smell of the beholder. Like mercury, "truth" is hard to pin down. It appears solid until you or someone else manipulates it through their own filters. We absorb so much information through our senses, our highly evolved brains make sense of it, and we then either pass it on, store it, or negate it. As we evolve into adults, most of us have few choices in terms of what we bring into that very vulnerable and impressionable place: our souls.

Peace and happiness depend upon how all the truths you are given resonate within your soul. External information lands somewhere within you, and at *that moment,* your truth is determined by your emotional reaction. This is where self-sabotage comes in, and where it can incapacitate us for a life of self-misconceptions and doubt. The truth you receive changes as it leaves you or anyone, embeds in someone or somewhere else, and morphs into a more prolific story or truth then was originally imprinted. Everything is nothing until it becomes something when someone breathes a version of their story into yet another version of the original. Our entire lives are spent disseminating stories told by someone else. It's time to listen to your own story, and more importantly figure out what your story should feel like.

Do liars always lie? Perhaps some are just storytellers that are unconcerned with the exact truth, favoring instead the effect of their stories. In the quest to gain and sustain personal happiness, consider being the wiser of the two, the narrator of a more factual story—the story closest to its origination. Enjoy the ride. Look at the truth as a beautiful aria, ebbing and flowing until it reaches a climax, only to start all over again when another truth hitches its wagon to *that truth.* Your hologram will take on a much more relaxed version when you decide truth is both finite and infinite, depending on the storyteller. And storytelling lies within all of us; some are just more practiced than others. Listen before acting. Determine if what you hear warrants a resting place in your soul. Change your soul diagram by understanding what to keep in your soul reservoir, and what to dismiss.

Chapter 3

Listen for Sound Quality

There have been times during deep discussions with a friend or a loved one that someone has asked, "If you had to pick once sense that you wouldn't want to live without, what would it be?" My answer is always *the sense of hearing*. With my sense of hearing intact, I can tell so much about all my surroundings and about people by receiving and processing sound waves. Every bit of my existence on this earth has been reinforced by sound and listening for clarity. In my early twenties, I suffered from a double ear infection and it lasted for over a month. That experience alone cemented my convictions about my most treasure sense. During that infection, my ears were ringing, sore, and plugged for six weeks, making me very agitated. I was without the navigation that I depended on for soul and life survival. The longer it went on, the grumpier I became. The double ear infection kept me from filtering and processing sound waves that made my life navigable, understandable, enjoyable, and fulfilling. Hearing well helps me in everything: coaching, professional speaking, sales/marketing, and writing. By listening to my audience—the breathing patterns, little utterances, cough, sighs, and laughs—I know if I am getting through to them. Every tiny soundwave alerts me as to whether I am motivating, inspiring, or am leaving them bored them to death. My acute hearing abilities have shaped who I am, which is why I listen for clarity through my hearing and all my other senses. Your senses shape your ability to know others and, more importantly, yourself. The soul reservoir needs all your senses to be alive and perceiving stimuli.

Our ability to know ourselves helps us filter what others are saying, or not saying, which helps keep negative vibes out of the soul reservoir. Absorbing the positive vibes from people, on the other hand, can most definitely shape and guide your performance, affecting your personal happiness. As you know, many people we encounter daily may not be mentally, emotionally, physically, psychologically, or spiritually healthy, spewing negative chemistry in our directions. Consider your workplace and coworkers. Sadly, many of us will actively listen and absorb the *negative chemistry* versus the positive chemistry of the messaging in space. Why? Because from the beginning, our surroundings are often systems designed to reinforce the negative versus the positives. Imagine how we'd all feel and be if the opposite reinforcements were true!

For instance, consider a work performance review where the rating possibilities are 1-5, but your employer/boss assigns you a 3.5 because "no employee ever gets a perfect five out of five." The judgment is made without valid rationale. Growing up, we are often corrected, sometimes harshly, for mistakes, or chastised for exerting our individualistic side. Society, peers, adults, siblings, and parents begin to denounce and reinforce fear about what they have been taught to believe is negative behavior or is— at least—a behavior or pattern misaligned with their own thinking. Remember your youth. Do you remember more of the positive or *the negative messaging?*

Just imagine if the opposite had been true and the messaging, we absorbed was powerfully positive and helpful. How would we feel about ourselves today? Emotionally, where would we be? Even those who are sensitive enough to be acutely aware of every stream of chemistry entering the emotional hemisphere might remember only the negative messages. Some messages can steer us, as most of us inherently want to be better. So, we tend to constantly remind ourselves of what we *didn't do correctly* by dipping into the familiar reservoir that makes us feel natural and comfortable.

Active listening, as defined by the **Business Dictionary:**
The act of mindfully hearing and attempting to comprehend the meaning of words spoken by another in a conversation or speech. Activity listening is an important business communication skill, and it can involve making sounds that indicate attentiveness, as well as t listener giving feedback in the form of a paraphrased rendition of what has been said by the other party for their confirmation. (Business Dictionary)

We all have much to learn by active listening, deciding personal truths for ourselves by weighing our own beliefs, value system, or truths against what we are hearing from others, or the way we feel when we hear incoming messages. It's important to "feel" the information versus just absorbing it. Your entire repertoire of skills is improved when you begin to truly listen to people, understanding what is going on around them, and consciously deciding what to let in and what to let pass by. The better you are at monitoring your senses and absorbing "choice" information (or chemistry), the purer your soul will be. That's not to say we don't all require constructive information along the way; we most certainly do.

For instance, children tend to listen actively. What children hear is processed immediately because all stimulation is new. Children are the best active listeners. While you may think they aren't paying attention, they are completely absorbing your words as energy flying through the air. Likewise, children absorb nonverbal communication better than you know. For children, and for most adults, what we hear determines how our emotions are gauged, and what our next move will be. We will base many of our future actions, behaviors, feelings, and emotions on how someone else felt or thought about us, essentially becoming someone else's soul chemistry, *until we realize we aren't*. This is somewhat like codependence, but it drives deeper physiologically.

Listening to music—experiencing sound waves created by voices and instruments—can have a compelling effect on us. Music can soothe the savage beast, uplift a deeply depressed person, or bring tears to someone grieving the loss of a loved one. Someone grieving the loss of their spouse may be moved to tears by the sound of their wedding song. Reliving a decision to self-harm or self-neglect based on information you absorbed from a wounded uncleansed soul can trigger an ill effect, as well. I named this chapter Listening for Sound Quality, and the previous one Truth Be Told because, as adults, it is our job to listen, filter, and cleanse the truth we host, and ultimately live much happier lives.

When writing, I must be able to clearly listen to my thoughts and emotions to bring the messages from inside of me onto the keyboard. Choosing to actively listen to others is a skill we can gain after years and years of practice, listening to every verbal and nonverbal message. There will always be noise to tune out, and some noise we just can't handle. I feel the soul of a dead animal on the side of the road and consciously must let it go to stay calm inside my own body and mind. Noise, energy, sound, information, nonverbal messaging, chemistry, emotions, feelings are all entering our senses all the time. At this moment, a little fan is blowing on my face to keep the air moving, making a soft motor sound. I hear every turn of the blade. We are rarely free of sound just like we are never free of the deluge of messages from everyone and everything around us daily. Being aware of who you are can only begin when you are aware of what you are bringing into your emotional dispatch and into the soul reservoir. The next time you get a bad vibe from someone, say these six words: "Your soul chemistry is not mine."

The energy that comes from millions of exchanges—spoken words from another's soul diagram, attempting to reach our emotional dispatch—will be absorbed by an active listener. Listeners must work diligently, even hyper-vigilantly, to pay attention to the words, sounds, feelings and emotions of another's human experience, staying cognizant of who you are, and keeping what others think and feel from polluting your soul reservoir. Each encounter can change, imprint, tarnish, or distort the soul diagram. <u>Do Not Enter</u> isn't just for construction zones.

Words are not a mere line-up of subject/verb/predicate. There is most always an *intended* message, sense, feeling or emotion for the active listener. Along the way, you've probably heard unkind words or feelings directed at you, such as, "you are really a lazy person," or "man, are you ugly!" The combined energy of something so damning and horrific can be launched in your direction, forcing you to deal with it the best way you know how. What we say to ourselves and others, and what we receive into our emotional dispatch, is critical to a life of happiness or a life of discomfort. Words have consequences when both spoken and received, so be careful interacting with others. Emotional abuse absorbed in any form creates a continual self-abuse cycle and every day thereafter we use that emotion as a gauge of our self-esteem.

The clothes I wear, the car I drive, or the companion I have on my arm is not as exhilarating and important to me as the condition of my soul. As a Life Coach, I can see how your soul has imprinted on your hologram, which is your face. I can see it on myself each day when I look in the mirror. If I am cycling through traumatic words I've carried from earlier in my life, or harmful present actions, my hologram is less bright and more weighted. Our holographic image or light will shine through our faces, and our face will emit energy that could potentially light up the room! We must first do the work of learning to like *who we are* versus what someone else scribed for us to be. Hopefully, you will have learned to love yourself as much or more.

The lessons in this chapter are critical in helping us reach our purest hologram. While I believe each chapter is just as fun and critical, the lessons about listening carefully and keeping the positive and dispelling the negative out of our emotional dispatch are especially crucial to our overall infinite soul's health.

Personal happiness is a personal project. It only works when we choose to actively listen and discern whether what we're hearing is from another person's soul or from our own. Sure, we could choose to only listen to our thoughts, embarking on a happy life within our narrow scope, gleaning only the necessary information from the noise entering our emotional sphere, or we can choose to listen well and learn more, gathering pertinent decision-making information from many sources and avenues that can potentially empower and sustain our happiness. As we navigate this life, we all must realize true personal happiness comes from truly listening to our soul, one that is aching for quality input leading to—and confirming—the personal truth of who we are. As soon as you can, learn to listen to the soul murmurings.

Words can carry emotional tags. Imagine all words are black and white, and all emotions that come along for the ride are a color. Now imagine your soul as a reservoir, or melting pot, for those emotions. Each black or white word creates an emotion, and each emotion enters your soul through those words, context, and meaning. For example, if someone said, "you're fat," those harsh words create a color, perhaps purple, representing self-consciousness. If I hear words of anger, you can bet the color would be red. Unfortunately, long before we are capable and can filter "the noise or colors" and the negative impact of ill-gotten mistruth, misperception, or hurtful words and behaviors from others, our soul reservoir begins to fill with all sorts of emotional colors. We fill with emotions, even by neglect or lack of nurturing. And often the question is, "Am I good enough?"

☼

At 18, I left home for college but immediately detoured to a psychiatrist's office that I'd found in the yellow pages. I explained to him, "I have many questions about how I feel after 18 years, and I want to talk about it."

I'll never forget his face and words as he whizzed backward in his wheeled office chair. "I've never had an 18-year-old come into my office and say something like this, please begin."

I wanted to talk about my childhood, shag old beliefs about myself, and begin the healing of my soul prior to my new life in college. Could I change the color of the liquid in my soul's reservoir, making it more positive, light, and beautiful, in *one day*? Nope, not in a single day. But if we know that our reservoir is filled with impurities and misinformation that we know aren't good for us, the only way to change that is to bring in new, pure unadulterated, and happy emotions. Talking about the condition of my self-worth with the psychiatrist helped me begin that journey of purification and redefinition. That day was the first and best step I had ever taken towards self-help, and I did it *in an instant*. Opening up to my doctor began the soul-cleansing I needed, bringing the standing liquid in my reservoir back to neutral or clear. Sure, I brought words with emotions to the psychiatrist, but I brought more than speech; I handed him an 18-year-old soul, laden with a ton of emotions about growing up in a home filled with a ton of emotional nuances.

As humans with amazing cognitive abilities, it's our duty to stand at guard (like at Buckingham Palace) at the emotional dispatch center, making sure nothing impure, ugly, hurtful, negative, manipulative, unhealthy, misguided, tainted, slanted, or untruthful steps foot onto the pad. Once there, those unwelcome elements are absorbed into

27

emotions which journey to the one place you must keep sacred: your soul. That place must be calm, peaceful, happy, pure, and healthy to live a life of happiness.

While I wouldn't want to lose the sense of sight (though at least then I would not be able to see a disturbing scene), it's harder to block out noise. As I am writing right now, I hear birds chirping, cars on their way to work on the distant highway, the pecking of my fingers on the keyboard, the sound of my own thoughts, the morning school bus going by, and the distant bark of a dog waiting for breakfast. All those are entering my world, and none of it affects my soul negatively. Now, I've shut my windows, put on some music, and all those other sounds are gone. That is how easy it can be when we are aware of what we want to absorb. Life can be beautiful when you choose to allow what lands in your emotional dispatch. Is it possible to stop the entire negative flow? No, we aren't islands, but nothing surpasses setting up an emotional sphere the way YOU want it to be. You direct the outcome of your emotional day.

Our hologram—our face—is hardwired to the soul, so bring in the good stuff! Some holograms carry so much pain that one's face affects people around them in a negative way. Don't let that be your story. Maybe pain and anger *are in your reservoir*, keeping those emotions may not serve you well. We must work to keep the reservoir pure, clean, and healthy.

Chapter 4

The Clean Reservoir

When you take care of what's on the inside (your soul), happiness will reflect through and on your face. What we learn from an early age may or may not be who we really are or want to be. On occasion, I'll tell people that I am working on a book, and they ask what I'm writing about. I'll relay the first two sentences of this chapter, and without exception every single person understands their message. We all are more than what we learned in our youth. That is why, when a soul reservoir is cleansed, the soul will function as a healthy strong place from which to draw decision-making and strength of character.

Let's address how *not* to have an emotional explosion and a lifetime of doubt and unhappiness. When we are confronted with a decision or a choice our soul reservoir is tapped for information, past emotions, and feelings to guide our life. Each draw provides the chemistry to fuel your emotional self. Once you realize that the soul is the foundational navigational system for your happiness, the freedom and clarity gained from cleansing it will become particularly important to you. How you feel about who you are comes from what we host inside of our soul, and we carry those emotions around with us like our last five-dollar bill. We use the soul reservoir daily to function. If the reservoir is not tended to, our happiness cannot be authentic, ever.

Imagine a pliable thin hose extended between the emotional dispatch and soul reservoir, almost like an intravenous line used in a hospital setting, dripping whatever chemistry is coming down that line. When you are called upon to function in your daily life, to take on more or to battle for your emotional happiness, or protect your mental or physical safety, the soul reservoir is what you tap into. If it's tainted, diluted, or consists of pure sludge keeping it unhealthy, there is personal work you must do. Some of us will do the work and some of us will continue to carry it around as-is. I've been working on mine since first feeling that something inside me wasn't aligned with my true self. I was a happy, positive, fun-loving person, but that's not what I exuded in my private quiet time. To the world I showed a smile and won each battle, but my soul was ailing with sadness and a longing for connections. I was functioning from a place of low self-esteem, self-hate, lack of trust, and doubt instead of confidence and conviction. I was a melting pot of so many mixed messages, emotions, and tribulations. I truly didn't know who this person in the mirror was. But I did know that it wasn't Anne!

When the reservoir is filled with negative emotional chemistry, your external energy or hologram will display sadness and unhappiness. You want the reservoir to be filled with happy, blessed feelings of gratitude, contentedness, kindness, peace, love, humility, positive, supportive, healthy, fulfilled, fun, and self-assured emotional sustenance. All the positive emotions are clear liquids and beautiful colors. Non-positive emotions also host a color, but theirs is a dark, dingy, weighted color. Emotions are a chemistry and energy that carry a weight, a viscosity, and a color. Until you do the work to purify the soul, those emotions and feelings will come along with you for the ride. It's time to let them go.

When the reservoir is filled with negative colors or chemistry it will be almost impossible to project happiness through your hologram because it cannot draw anything positive from the reservoir. It is like going to a grocery store and filling up your grocery basket with only carbohydrates. Chances are you won't find anything healthy in a bag of crackers and a box of those glazed donuts. So, essentially, the adage of "what you eat, you are" applies, because what you take in via your soul, you will become. The difference between soul and body? Your soul takes a personal hit while you use that bad or negative information, and you'll never cleanse the negative out of your soul, feeling forever less than happy. Those around you will not want to be with you.

We believe what we are taught, told, and hear. Some adults who were tortured as a child cannot overcome the impact of the experience on their soul. Our self-awareness and outlook start in our emotional dispatch center (think of it as a high-dive platform), heads down to the soul reservoir, filling up, and then eating away at the lining of the soul reservoir. From there, with every experience we encounter in life we draw from the original imprint we absorbed deep within our soul and sadly that may be in some form of self-abuse, self-neglect or anger. Anything negative that you secretly do on a daily basis to yourself, or any negative thought pattern you repeat, comes from your soul. *Only you* can find that emotion you adopted inadvertently, and only *you* can cleanse your soul.

At any given moment on any given day or circumstance we can draw emotional energy from our soul diagram. I was in a Vinyasa Yoga class once. We were in our final stages of relaxation and as we were all coming out of our silence, some of the ladies started packing up their things. Another yogi in the class started talking about her newly arrived baby daughter. She seemed to me to be beyond baby-making years, and I hadn't seen her appear pregnant. I assumed she was referring to a successful adoption. She was talking about how her 4-year-old daughter and new daughter would relate. I began to silently weep. Tears were flowing down my cheeks. Just 12 years before, I lost my daughter four days before she would have been born. The emotions held inside my soul reservoir from that experience are utter pain and sadness. Hearing someone talk about a new baby, and being unable to stop the information from entering my emotional dispatch, made it impossible to not revisit and relive my feelings of loss. The mere fact I was childless was too much to bear at that moment. I have not completely cleansed my reservoir of that memory or its emotions, so it will always remain a difficult thought for me to endure. I may have to carry it with me until I pass, or until I come to grips, or reframe it in my heart, head, and soul. I took a picture of myself after that class and realized just how much that subject affected my hologram. The experience in yoga class caused my hologram to look just like it did the day the doctor took my daughter's still body from my tummy. At that class and to this day, I feel distraught, bewildered, empty, and so incredibly sad. All those emotions were allowed into my emotional dispatch the day my daughter passed, and they remain hosted in my reservoir. The important lesson in this story is, I can let this negativity ultimately find a permanent spot on my soul diagram, or I can choose to work on eradicating the pain and sadness from my soul.

One sure way to keep your reservoir from filling up with negative emotions is to NOT let them into emotional dispatch. As simple as it may sound, it is difficult to achieve that level of skill. It can happen so quickly when, for instance, someone says something that sounds condescending. Most humans tend to want to understand why something is happening. If your first waking thoughts are drawn from the negative chemistry simmering in your reservoir, and you haven't done the personal work to cleanse, your entire day might just be shit. We begin the negative tape loop immediately in the morning to maintain control or some sense of familiarity and comfort. Too often, it's easier to be comfortable in the muck, rather than lifting ourselves up and out of it and making necessary changes. It's always your choice: continue being a slave to unhappiness and a mule carrying the emotional chemistry you inherited around with you, or decide to offload the negative and make room for the positive.

When we bring information into emotional dispatch, we begin the mental gymnastics. Sometimes we rationalize it, justify it, change it, manipulate it, distort it, disagree with it, agree with it, or share it. But whatever we do with the information, we've started the process of sending it to the soul reservoir. This is where we have to say, out loud, "STOP! You there… negative unhealthy information… STAY OUT! NO WAY will I let you in here. No way will I let this process of depression begin!"

I am getting better at it, but still there are those days when my outlook is negative, and I feel physically and emotionally depleted. Caught in those moments, my best friend will ask, "Are you thinking bad thoughts?" Bless his heart. The truth is, I am allowing myself to feel crappy and emotionally wounded from things that happened to me as an innocent being, instead of feeling strong in who I am today!

I shared the story about my yoga class experience and losing my daughter because I have not thoroughly cleansed my reservoir of that horrific and negative experience. You may have similar experiences that need cleansing. For some reason, I enjoy dipping into the cesspool of emotions surrounding the loss of my daughter, and I believe it has to do with the connection (or the safe place) where we have our last time and space. Does it serve me? Maybe, but probably not well. While those emotional experiences take place less often, I'm still a long way from being completely "cured" of them. Now, When I hear the word "baby" or "newborn," I cry one out of ten times as opposed to ten in ten times. When the subject comes up, it still amazes me how many women will say, "I lost a daughter too." How kind and loving women can be, sharing a connection, reminding me that I am not alone, and igniting the chemistry in my reservoir that helps cleanse my soul, and returns me to a purified and glorious hologram.

We all have those experiential reminders of emotions we carry around with us from many, many years ago. Cleansing the soul is a process by which you either remove or dilute the current reservoir of the negative chemistry by which our hologram develops and responds. You won't be perfect at it right away, but you will improve over time. Our time here is short; the longer you wait to get started, the harder it will become to change. Think of this as an extremely healthy diet for the soul. Let's look deep within our soul reservoir, identifying and touching those deprecating emotions that are key to our emotional intelligence. Begin to parse out which memories drain energy from you and leave those that infuse positive energy.

When possible, only allow those thoughts into emotional dispatch that will support, serve and uplift your emotional and mental state to a positive place. A positive attitude frames our outlook in a way where we will feel light, upbeat, happy, fun, loving and free, originating from a positive reservoir.

Remember the story of my fourth-grade teacher who humiliated me and two other girls? I was a sweet, innocent, tall and happy kid. You may be empathizing with me right now, thinking about something that happened to you, and asking how I replaced the emotion of self-loathing and poor self-body image with love and respect. Using the action steps outlined below, I replaced my self-loathing with self-care. Now I ask myself, *Will today be a day that is full of healthy activities and food intake?* My immediate internal answer is, *"Absolutely."* Now, when I must weigh in at the doctor's office, the old emotions of fear, anxiety and stress have been *replaced* with self-control, ideal weight check, and *my choice* to weigh.

Now, it's your turn. Pick a reoccurring thought pattern that wreaks havoc on your nervous system and do away with the lies and distortions that someone outside of yourself, or some event, placed upon you when you were unaware that you had control of how you feel.

Wisdom Points:

Reject Button. Reject incoming traffic/noise/pollutants, negative words, or energy by using what I call the "reject button" method. The minute you suspect bad chemistry coming your way, within seconds and within your mind, hit a huge red and black "REJECT" button, slamming it as hard as you can. Don't allow the thoughts and chemistry to enter the emotional dispatch area. By now, you know what the thought patterns are that ruin and run your life so… *HIT IT! REJECT!*

Drop Kick. This is a visual for those sneaky thoughts that make their way into emotional dispatch. You'll know it when it happens because you'll think negative thoughts and spiral down to depression and unhappiness. As an example, let's use "I am not worthy." Think about the emotion that occurs when you think of that phrase, position your feet shoulder length apart, get in a good stance, and wind up your power leg and drop kick those non-serving emotions into the atmosphere. Place those emotions inside of a big red rubber playground ball and set it down right in front of that power leg. Imagine kicking that ball so hard it evaporates into dust, never to return. Or for the golfers in the bunch, have you ever seen someone hitting golf balls into an ocean or lake? Like drop-kicking, get that perfect swing, follow through, and launch that golf ball into the ocean, never to be found again. Seriously, take a golf ball and send it sailing Visualize that emotion of unworthiness and drive that sucker to oblivion. The mind is such a powerful tool. Get up and do it!

Replace. When your soul reservoir hosts an all-too familiar negative chemistry, it's time to replace it with new chemistry. Let's say the negative chemistry is insecurity from years of manipulation and verbal abuse from an alcoholic parent or narcissistic partner. (Only you know what emotions you carry around daily.) Go on a hunt. Become the predator, finding all lingering negative chemistry, gathering it up, and replacing it with brand new chemistry. Find positive thoughts that dispel any negative emotions and start a new mantra with specific words and emotions that you want, such as purity, peace, calm, normalcy, integrity, and morality. If you were molested as a child, find those emotions, memories and beliefs, replacing them with the fact you are now a stronger, healthier person. Now, you will only love and honor your body, forever. Replace it and let it go! The abuser doesn't deserve your energy and your reservoir doesn't need to host the bad chemistry. Not now. Not today. Never! The negative experience can be anything. We all have something we need to let go of, something that doesn't serve us well. Replace it.

Saturate it. The process for coping with what has happened throughout your life, or what continues to happen, is more intimate, and thus a more intricate process is called for. I like to call this wisdom point, "saturating it." For some of us, making sense or coming to grips with past injuries to our soul requires covering the same ground over and repeatedly. Some write, some speak, some speak and write, some journal, go to therapy, have a support group, a mentor, a secret friend, a neighbor who will listen, an affair, a private addiction, a covert self-neglecting or abuse… This step of saturating the chemistry is, frankly, one of the simpler choices. By diving in head first with a therapist, life coach, or great friend, the attention and energy you give to the negative emotion will thin the viscosity of the chemistry, and you will become stronger while the negative emotion becomes weaker, eventually clearing bad chemistry. The only problem with the wisdom of saturating is that the problem is always there, like standing water. The more you let standing water sit, the smellier it becomes. You are already compromised, and it is hard to discern what is best. You may not always choose the best form of "therapy" to dissolve the negativity from your reservoir. Be careful on this one. I know people who use addiction as a tool, but it is only a substitute for what is really going on. Deciding to saturate the process and taking years to find the real issue and annihilate it, might not be the best way, but it is, one way.

Frame It. For others suffering from a "one-time" deluge from a negative experience, I'd like to call this wisdom point, "frame it." Imagine a picture frame—any color you choose. Take the face, the experience, the object, or the organization that hurt you and place it in that frame. Clean your reservoir of bad ju ju by *replacing* that picture with one that represents your soul takeaway from the experience. For example, if you were fired from an organization for no reason, take the name of that company and put it on YOUR WALL OF FAME of lessons learned. From that horrible experience you've either learned something about yourself, or about them, that represents an exceptional find, a Great Learning Experience.

☼

I was fired from a company due to internal politics. I'd made high sales and interacted well with peers and customers, but the fact that I was well-liked and popular was seen by my boss as a threat. No one liked her at all, so the support and admiration that my colleagues had for me irritated the heck out of her. I should have been leading the team of salespeople, but my inner and outer beauty was a huge threat to her, as she landed her job because she was a friend of another manager there. I have since then put that woman and that company in a frame on my wall of fame. For me, a picture of those times reminds me of how miserable and controlling she was as a human and boss, and how oppressive that situation was for me. I didn't like myself during that time. I was trying to change to fit my boss's needs, and I surely didn't want that for the rest of my working life. Being let go was an absolute gift, a huge burden lifted. I take that emotion of "not good enough" and FRAME it within the knowledge that I deserved much better. See how I turned that around?

Own it. This may be hard if you've done the dirty deed of hurting someone for your own self-preservation. You must live with that, and your soul reservoir chemistry will be forever altered until you own it or admit what you did to your spouse, children, coworker, friend, etc. In owning it, you get to the core of what you did, and why you did it, so you can release the guilt and find peace. Harboring guilt will never amount to happiness; it is the acid that erodes all other chemistry, surfaces, walls, and tissue. Own it, make it right, and get rid of it. Throw it out in the trash and put it behind you. One sure way is to write an apology letter but never send the letter. I believe that sending the letter could do more harm than good, but if you do, be ready for a rebuttal. More importantly, understand that the healing comes from writing down everything you feel surrounding the certain subject or emotion. Continued rationalization or non-exposure of something so heavy is never a substitute for owning the wrongdoing and will only serve as a crunch in denial land.

Make Friends With It. Have you ever heard the phrase, "Keep your friends close and your enemies closer?" You have an intimate relationship with that emotion, and, for some reason, you choose to let it serve you. The self-abuse from smoking or drinking to your own detriment is a mask for the real issue. Many may say, "I like to smoke," or "I only drink socially." Like I said, I don't recommend making a deal with the friend devil because you'll end of disliking how you feel, and your hologram will not reflect a pure and contented soul. You'll eventually want to select another wisdom point because it takes time for some to own something you do to hurt yourself.

Burn It or Blow It Up! I once took everything that haunted me—words people spoke, actions people took, things that happened to me, hardships, losses, anything I could think of—and wrote it all down on a piece of paper. I started a huge bonfire in the backyard and burned up every single bad-energy memory or chemistry that I was hosting in my soul, along with any hurts I may have caused others. I cleansed my soul right out! Something physical and spiritual as a fire or explosion is pretty moving! But please practice safety!

Bottom line: If negative chemistry in your soul is lingering, lounging, bubbling, and doesn't serve you in a positive healthy way, you'll want to extract it, dilute it, purge it, kill it, befriend it or send it sailing. Sooner or later, you must make room only for reservoir chemistry that supports you in the healthiest of ways. If what you carry around doesn't serve you, do not allow it to make a home in your soul reservoir, diagram—ultimately, your hologram.

Chapter 5

Eradicate Lying to Yourself and Others

I n chapter 2, I revealed that for personal happiness to prevail in our lives, we have to filter through the incoming chemistry, and our current reservoir, by exacting and knowing the origins of our emotional self. Emotions have a direct cause-and-effect relationship on self-talk and how we behave towards others. As a newly aware consumer of your soul reservoir, external messages should no longer enter if they don't serve you in becoming and being a healthy and productive human.

It's essential that you understand that soul cleansing is within your grasp. While you didn't ask for the information you own, you do carry it around like a faithful scout. If you wake up every day more concerned about how others feel about you, or worried if they approve of you, it's a good indication you still have work to do.

From my interaction with people as an empath and coach, I find that most are not genuinely happy or in what I call a "tranquil soul chemistry state." They are not physiologically calm. Many have over-extended themselves financially, spent their life in an unbalanced relationship, become addicted to some external emotional "feel good" activity, or made a habit of denying who they are out of fear they will be looked down on. Our hologram (our faces) are based on our soul diagram and the output of energy from many negative feelings and emotions we've learned through years of misdirection, misunderstanding, misguidance, and downright lies. Those messages tend to run on a constant thought-loop, dictating our every feeling. Additionally, we absorb other's excitement, depression, sadness, polluted energy, soul diagrams, and/or deficient interpretational view of their life. Their soul diagram and soul reservoir are not yours, yet people are very willing to push their negative emotions onto you. That must stop. And as soon as you know this, it *will* stop.

Those who impart messages of emotional pain and energy to unsuspecting people are often those closest to them in proximity or access. Consider mass killings; a murderer goes from being a loving child to committing vicious crimes. That child unwittingly picked up messages along the way that were not his or her own. The lack of nurturing or sound guidance from an authority figure creates obscurity, detachment, and disillusionment in the child. That state of being is a sad cycle of abuse, often started within familial, religious, and educational environments. Is the opposite true? Absolutely. A childhood spent in an environment with positive messaging and nurturing most likely resulting in a well-rounded, self-accepting, and empowered healthy adult.

As a child you may have been extremely mean to a sibling or a friend, for no reason at all. Those outbursts were affecting others because you lacked the love, nurturing, or direction you needed most, so lashing out seemed right. Another personality type that we've all seen: a person who brags a lot but has nothing substantial to back it up. Their life is void or limited in terms of what they consider to be important experiences, so they bleat noise, energy, and ill emotions and views based on their narcissistic, interpretational view of life. You may say to them, "Wow, how do you know so much about that?" They can rarely explain how they arrived at their opinion. If they only have one very narrow view of life, it's likely that their parents deadened their receptors prematurely by their own bloated, immature, view of life. *Look what we made, honey? Isn't he grand?*

As a smart consumer of information absorption, I work hard to understand what I am processing as *my* truth and what an *outside truth* is. We are receiving and sending messages all the time and filtering is an ongoing job, just as stopping the cycle of thoughts badgering your brain daily, also known as "baggage," that residual bad chemistry within our soul. You hear it in the dating world; would-be daters claim they don't want someone with baggage, yet they carry loads of their own. Often, the potential dater is hoping is that their date has done the personal work to become healthy emotionally, instead of having a jaded and hurtful view on everything.

In all types of relationships, each person carries the reservoir chemistry from the previous relationship, as well as their entire life of relationships, despite any hopes of "starting fresh." You cannot start fresh unless you make a conscious effort to cleanse your soul reservoir before you carry it into a relationship, especially a parent-child or romantic relationship.

That is why lying to oneself is one the biggest gigs going. You perpetuate what you have learned, which are often mistruths. What do I mean by "lying to oneself"? Let's define the word, because its definition is often crafted to suit our own personal fantasies or belief systems, which, by the way, *aren't our own* to begin with. Personal experience and long periods of introspection and dissection are the mother of a credible belief system and the ability to nurture others by true and helpful messaging. Being aware of your emotional footprint is necessary.

Anne's Definition of Lying:
Altering the truth for any reason. Truth may be your own interpretation, experience, or a view of something you've gleaned. Lying is changing the truth to suit a personal deep-seated motivation or deficit. It is the art of smoke-and-mirror communication mastery, used to gain an edge or platform from which to speak. Lying is a form of deception or embellishment for the sake of exaggeration or interpretation to suit one's own agenda.

Lying is used in all walks of life and, yes, everything coming at you is, without a doubt, smoke and mirrors. As soon as you are able, your job in life is to understand that you are receiving information that you must decipher as either smoke, or a smoke bomb. Consider radio talk show hosts, editors, disc jockeys and the like—anyone in a platform to speak or write and influence. They are spewing information to the public, laced with their interpretation of the world. News reporters on television put their emotional spin on the words they are reading. The mind deceives the soul so eloquently that hologram incongruence is the outcome. We don't know what we want or who we are! Listen with all your senses the next time you listen to or watch someone deliver the news. As unsuspecting humans, we either absorb or deflect what we see, here, feel, learn, and ultimately believe. As a child, surroundings are filled with reporters and newscasters telling us their view and take on life, right and wrong, good and evil. Once in emotional dispatch, we begin to base our personal belief systems and values on what we've gathered, been shown, taught, or *felt* in our every conscious moment.

A counselor once asked me, "What personal values do you want to base Anne's life on?" No one had ever approached me with such a thought-provoking question! I've talked with people who have their favorite talk show host right up there next to God and Family. They live and die by what they hear via radio or television, as if it was truth transcribed from a million years ago. Nothing learned from others should be deemed "gospel," because every person's soul diagram was scribed by their journey. You must learn to be the judge and imprinter of soul diagram (and ultimately hologram), and you'll know truth when you see, hear, and feel it.

Lying to ourselves… Let's take simplistic approach by discussing the self-deception, "I didn't eat that much." First, if you have to say that statement out loud, you DID eat too much! If you must protest something verbally, it's likely that your protestation isn't the entire truth. A good friend of mine and I sometimes talk about people who brag about their wealth or position in life, and how they usually don't possess what they are bragging about. The same applies to having a perfect, "love-filled" relationship. I've learned that women tend to lie about their weight, relationships, and age. Men tend to lie about their penis size, height, and financial position. Those who have it don't have to brag about it. Thus, saying that you "didn't eat that much" translates to a confession that you ate more than you planned, and now feel guilty.

One of my favorite self-written quotes is, "there are no alternatives to action" because when you are stuck in a bad cycle of mistruths, any action you can take, will result in motion and motion will create new emotions. So when you lie, you add more negative chemistry of disbelief to your soul reservoir making your decision making more tentative. Lying to yourself and others, puts deception in emotional dispatch. It is nothing more than a stall or de-motivational tactic and will promptly begin the entire cycle of soul cleansing. Taking action to understand and know yourself better than you ever have before, will stop the cycle of lying and will launch you forward to becoming very self-aware with a healthy hologram. You will just evolve and *become*. It takes a lot of discipline and work to stop the overt lying to yourself and others. Is anyone ever okay with admittance of something they may not be so proud of, the answer is deep down inside or maybe not so deep, NO!

Wishing for something *does not net you anything*. It's just air. People who say "I wish" or "I'll try" "or it's the truth" are practicing deception. That form of deception is the most harmful because it misleads the listener and it distorts your personal view of yourself. Self-actualization is best supported by taking steps that best serve you to become the person you want to be. You'll notice I said, "Best serves" you. It is your job to determine what "best serving you" means; prematurely projecting words is nothing more than a waste of good air. Have you ever heard someone say, "He doesn't say much at all, but when he does, it is always profound."? I'd rather be that guy than someone who belts out nonsense to make my emotional footprint, causing someone else to doubt what is or is not the best truth from the best source.

Lying to yourself disrupts the flow of good chemistry within your mind, body and soul. When you add an element of dishonesty, even if by your own creative storytelling, to the emotional dispatch center, the chemistry becomes tainted and journeys down to your soul reservoir, only to leave you with the challenge of cleansing and purifying your soul once again. So, stop lying to yourself and others. Find and embrace the truth, whether it be positive or negative, and handle it in its entirety. Then, truth will serve you in a positive healthy way. Start ahead of the game, not behind!

Have a discussion with yourself that eliminates all lies. Lazy minds will not challenge this aspect of their neuroses because it would take significant work to figure out where the lie originates, why it's perpetuated, and why it's carried around daily. It's work to carry around lies! Most likely, we will continue to use the lie to serve our inflated self-importance, or self-degradation, by living in a state of denial, which serves no one.

Addicts do this all the time. Interestingly, addicts know they are lying to themselves, but they choose the vice over personal growth and happiness, justifying the lie every chance they get. The chemistry of the drug, in conjunction with the polluted soul reservoir supporting the addictive behavior, is too powerful and controlling. So, the lie continues. Addiction is nothing more than one lie after another, changing and dominating a life.

I had a friend believed so strongly that he wasn't alcoholic that he would try to convince me by saying, "I drink a lot of water when I drink; a bottle of booze is nothing!" Or, "I grabbed a bottle and went to work, I wasn't *that* drunk-driving because I had eaten." He told so many lies, one after another. The final straw of our friendship came when he told me the truth: "I will never stop drinking." I was shocked and ended our friendship. Lying to himself and others caused the breakup of a good friendship and the demise of a human spirit and soul. I knew his father was an ass, and yet my friend never chose to deal with the emotional horror he suffered as a child. He was so hurt, sad, and frustrated
.

Allowing outside stimulus to dominate your soul reservoir will net you unhappiness. You cannot worship two gods. What you know and feel is right in your mind, heart, and soul is all that matters. Personal happiness begins with an acceptance that how you are and how your feel is a compilation and creation of influence and deception and there is always a reason to check in on how you are doing. When you lie to smooth over the uncomfortable agitations within your soul, you are simply perpetuating unhappiness.

During a session with a client one day, she told me why she was overweight. "When he [her partner] hit me," she said, "it was because he had anger issues. I understand why he did it." The victim was justifying the behavior of the abuser. Domestic abuse victims tell themselves this lie all the time, while the abuser tells himself that what he did wasn't that bad. The cycle of abuse continues. Stop the insanity. Get to the core of the issues and fix them once and for all for life!

In the third grade, I was caught for cheating on an SRA reading test. The teacher told my mom, for which I am thankful, since getting caught is one way of correcting bad behavior. My mom said to me, "What made you think that the person you cheated off of was smarter than you?" What a profound question! The sentiment has stayed with me forever. Somewhere along the line, I was given a message I believed and continued to lie to myself throughout life, that I was not good enough, or smart enough, to trust myself. There is no other lie more detrimental than that! Don't believe that someone else is smarter at your happiness than you are. You are the genius behind your happiness and nothing anyone else says can destroy that fire that burns within you. Only you can snuff out that flame, but others will try.

☼

Here are six attributes that reveal a lot about a person's hologram and soul reservoir. Think twice about having these in your life. It is up to you to detect these types of personalities and leave people who meet the descriptions standing at the curb.

They rarely give others credit unless it promotes their own status.

They steal and use your ideas, thoughts, or energy for their personal or professional agenda.

They ignore you completely because they believe they are better than you in every way.

They base their personal value system on their own judgments, experiences, and wealth, and use those values to compare and judge you.

Their favorite subject is their—or someone else's—wealth.

They are shallow, and never talk about anything deeper than their last purchase or someone else's choices.

Conversely, here are six things I value in a person's character and hope transfers to their hologram.

Their ability to be authentic and honest.

Their priorities line up with goodness and fairness.

They do their absolute best to be a good human and admit their mistakes when they make them.

To them, money is a tool, not a measurement.

The order of their output is self-care and generosity.

When they walk away from you, you wish they hadn't, but you are also left feeling happy.

44

Chapter 6

The Soul is Never for Sale

Historically, many people have sacrificed their lives for their beliefs and used religious differences as the "reason" for war, famine, and strife. If you seriously think about that concept, it seems ridiculous. We all believe in something amazing and vast, whether it is through the filter of one ideal or another.

The unfortunate part about humankind is that we are not on the same page at the same time, emotionally or mentally. Our soul reservoirs are pulsating, revving, and spewing at different thresholds and temperaments. If 20 people were gathered in a room, three or four might have 100% conviction in a belief, ready to fight to the death. The others might sit back and watch because they couldn't care less or have completely different feelings about the topic at hand. Of all those people gathered, how many do you think would stand up for what they believe? Sadly, most of us don't really know, with absolute certainty, what WE believe to be true, or if we believe in ourselves. It takes years to become who we truly are and then to be strong enough to stand up for what we genuinely believe. We know what we've been taught and what've we picked up along the way, but too often, we are not 100% sure of our beliefs.

As a speaker, coach, and writer, I challenge you to FEEL who you are first. Get to know yourself and better understand how you act *because of those feelings and* realize what you are sending out to the world via your soul chemistry. Your messages are indicative of your personal soul chemistry, derived from the condition of your soul reservoir. In other words, you are what you host!

Life happiness is only as good as our soul reservoir's condition. The world taught me that I was (physically) a big, ugly monster. If I don't do the work of cleansing those emotions from my reservoir, I'll never think much of myself or have a good self-body

45

image. I challenge you to think about your life, your choices, and the condition of your soul on a daily basis because true happiness comes from aligning your decisions with who you truly are, not from what others and the world have taught you to believe about yourself. I give us all permission to *obsess* about who we really are, and why. If we won't gauge the temperature and the purity of our soul reservoir, who will? Only we can do the cleansing. Check the soul reservoir often so you stay focused, healthy, and can give great self-care and affect others in a positive way. Are the low self-esteem issues you carry every waking moment your own, or are they someone else's?

Ask yourself right now, "What am I feeling at this moment inside my soul? Does what I believe cause me trouble in my thinking daily? What's at the core of my not-so-calm physiological and emotional state I live within myself each day? Is what I host my truth or someone else's truth? Am I living in a constant state of panic, listening to an inner voice that says I am not worthy?" Looking at the world through an emotional state of "I am not worthy of love" versus "I am worthy of love" are really two different vantage points. Can you relate to why it is so important to know where your current emotional state comes from and why do you continue to host it?

Our souls are not for sale. The most disruptive, self-doubting and sad times in my life were when I allowed something or someone to invade the tranquility of what I knew to be true about myself, and what was best for me. I sold off a piece of my soul for their interest (or due to their insecurity), killing a part of myself, and allowing a part of them to live within my reservoir. With enough courage, we can find our way back, ridding ourselves of others' soul chemistry and filling our reservoir with good emotional sustainable chemistry.

Don't ever sell off a piece of your soul or allow your soul to be infiltrated with pollutants that do not aid or serve you in a healthy, positive way. People everywhere around you will deluge you with crazy, fixed notions, informational dialogues and practices, beliefs, and stories because they are unaware, or too lazy, to fix their own issues before imprinting onto others. Your soul is the foundational navigation system of your life, providing all the proper coping skills to live happily and successfully. Your soul's condition determines whether you linger, flounder, and wallow in doubt, self-destruction, self-pity, or pain. The soul fills your face with light and love, or sadness and pain. It's truly that simple. When people say, "Get out of your own way," or "Get out of your head," that's pointing to the self-deprecation born of bad chemistry you're carrying and accustomed to tapping into. If you are a sensitive soul, as I am, everything could have affected you a lot harder than you know.

Working on cleansing the soul and never selling any piece of your soul is paramount to living a happy life. If you look in the mirror and you are not comfortable with who you are, what you see, the choices you've made, or the position you are in, start looking inward, instead of outward, for the most truthful answers. Are you hosting the chemistry from someone else's soul reservoir? Is your hologram yours, or someone else's? If you realize part of your soul's real estate is being held captive by misinformation, it's time to CLEANSE! If you believe something to not be true about yourself, expose it and rid yourself of that belief that was never true in the first place. It is no longer yours to carry around every day.

The foundation of your soul consists of its original composition (i.e., genetics) and chemistry from conception to today. Just because you are in the womb doesn't mean there isn't information flowing to your soul. We must become aware of what is entering our emotional dispatch before we let it reach our soul reservoir, and we don't have to *see* something to know if it is emotionally welcoming, crippling, uplifting, or discrediting. Instead, it's the "feelings" or the "vibes" that we get when we are around someone. Those don't stop just because we're in the womb or 99 years old. That flow of influence begins in the moment of conception. The safest and purest time of your soul reservoir is prior to anyone knowing that you have been created. For a split second, your soul exists in a state of absolute purity without any new emotional chemistry to distort perfect harmony. When the moment of dispatch happens, we begin receiving unwanted and polluted chemistry and our soul begins to fill. Now that you are more cognizant of your soul, when you think a part of your soul is about to be sold off, you'll stop it dead in its tracks. Keep unwanted and unhealthy feelings from infiltrating and taking over a piece of healthy real estate in your soul reservoir.

Having lived a full and extraordinary life, there are certain truths I have vetted, have total clarity on because, I have given life my all, fought my way up and out, and have no regrets about what I stand on today. We will all face obstacles and challenges along the way, and we all want authentic, bright, and congruent holograms. Being true to yourself and allowing nothing to enter or little to enter emotional dispatch that will contradict your personal value system is critical to overall happiness. Living, feeling, and being able to speak your emotional truth is the ultimate goal and the outcome that will affect everyone around you in a positive and healthy way.

When you sell your soul, you'll have an uneasiness that lingers. Selling your soul will feel similar like walking home alone from school as a child. Remember walking home on a sunny or cloudy day and how it felt to be completely alone? It would have been so nice to have someone to walk with home with, but until you reached home, you had to deal with feelings of loneliness, insecurity and uncertainty. Perhaps there was a scary house, a creepy person, or the questionable insane dog that was always lurking, ready to lunge. Maybe a strange vehicle passed. Did it stop? Is it turning around? While your goal was to get home safely, have a snack, and play, you first had to walk past every nuisance along the way. Home was the destination of safety and familiarity.

The walk towards emotional happiness and calmness is based on a personal journey of self-discovery that will be shorter and more comfortable than the walk home. Just keep reminding yourself that you can't sell any part of our soul for the sake of someone else's values or propositions. When you reject the unhealthy emotional quagmire of information coming into your emotional dispatch center, you are doing what is best for you. The longer you ignore the discrepancy in your soul, the longer it will keep you agitated and incongruently unauthentic. (Refer to chapter four to begin cleansing your reservoir.) If you picked something up as a child that limits healthy thinking and behavior, the sooner you understand it, the sooner you will find happiness. I'm not a big, ugly monster but believe me, there are times and days when I dip my toe into that feeling so I can feel like myself again, because somewhere along the line I believed that message.

I continue to work with people who look to external sources such as the opposite sex, money, toys, big purchases, pornography, drugs, alcohol, smoking, masturbation, and food, to name a few, for temporary fixes, keeping the soul reservoir chemistry the same, and potentially making it worse with self-loathing. We all must ask ourselves the tough questions and do the work to become physiologically calm.

Begin the awareness process by recognizing that strange, uneasy feeling as it enters your emotional dispatch center. It's your duty to make the necessary deviations and corrections in the course so you can live a fully functioning happy life. If you don't, there will be no one to blame but yourself.

Here is a list of behaviors that indicate that your soul might be slipping away:

Continuing to hurt yourself and others by your words, actions, lack of action, or neglect
Staying in a job that is completely not *you* and makes you unhappy
Living in a home environment that is detrimental to your personal health and growth
Staying in a relationship that doesn't benefit you, or that you know isn't right for you
Going to college without truly giving it your 100% best effort (Doing anything without giving it your all, for that matter!)

Actively and conscientiously being a criminal, thief, adulterer, mean person, conniving, manipulating, or controlling type of person, and, despite admitting it to yourself and others, never doing anything to own or change the behaviors

Not learning and growing, or refusing to better yourself or become better for your family or children

Never obtaining outside knowledge or counsel because you think you know it all and don't need any help

Always having to be right and never saying you're wrong or apologizing to others

Not trying something new because of stubbornness

Never truly growing or questioning, but solely accepting and basing your life and behavior on the information you obtained from 0-18 years of age

Isolating yourself to continue self-abusive behaviors

Never allowing for positive outside influence

Chapter 7

The Next Hold - Why Challenges in Life Exist

There will be continuous challenges throughout life. We should expect a lot of them! Consider rock climbers—some of the most courageous people on the planet—who suspend themselves in midair, hanging by ropes and karabiners. (Or nothing at all; do or die!) What an incredible feat. For me, crossing a bridge over a river, 20 feet above the water, makes me nervous. My knees begin to buckle and my tummy goes into my throat. Imagine the mental and physical strength it takes to plant your hands on a less-than-desirable hold in midair, lifting your body and hoisting your entire self upward without looking back or down. All the while, you're hoping that those ahead of you or behind you are doing their jobs as well. Climbing takes enormous concentration, personal strength and agility, and it appears that these types of courageous individuals are on top of the world. They harness barely any fear because they have mastered the skills to be exactly where they are, just like you'll be when it comes to mastering what lives in your soul reservoir, on your soul canvas and, ultimately, the hologram!

Mastering the skills of knowing what to allow into your emotional dispatch center and mastering the climb up and out of the depths of inauthenticity and incongruent mind-body behaviors, is the essence of my work and book. Life is beautiful when you know who you truly are inside, and the hologram will shine brightly every day. Life is enough of an adventure for most of us so suspending ourselves into midair on the side of a mountain isn't necessary, but metaphorically, it is. Digging to the depths of your uneasiness in life isn't the greatest learning curve or lesson. Life, as well as reintroducing yourself to who you know you are, can be scary or truly liberating depending on how far we have let our soul reservoir go in a direction that doesn't serve us. Life will throw us all huge curves and disappointments and at times will completely knock us off our

51

base. But after you do the work and cleanse your soul those huge curves and disappointments will be more of a ripple than a Bermuda Triangle.

Life has been my mountain day after day, day in and day out. Just as in rock climbing, when cleansing your soul reservoir, start with one emotion or feeling, start with *one small climb*. Touch one area that keeps you living a less than beautiful life. The crucial key is starting slowly, working your way to those emotions you host, until you become skilled in the cleansing process. I am certain climbers don't start out climbing the highest summit on their list of destinations. They likely start at the local mall's rock-climbing wall! So, start with one emotion inside your soul reservoir. Choose one, maybe it's *not feeling worthy* of anyone or not feeling good for whatever reason. Choose one reoccurring feeling you are ready to address. My initial deep dive at 18 years old was, "Did I deserve to be made to feel bad about being me?"

It's important to set the scene regarding your personal journey to the depths of understanding your soul reservoir. There is a certain strength and endurance it will take to face some of the personal issues you've been lugging around for all these years. Addressing the obstacles and soul cleansing needed will be that next hold of self-worth and emotional freedom—a journey you may face alone.

Just as a climber is always looking for that next hold, you too must look at your personal obstacle (soul cleansing) as your next hold in life to getting to know your true self. Knowing you have the skills and tools you need to overcome that next obstacle or self-awakening experience life puts in your way will keep you calm as you approach the challenge. Knowing who you truly are is the purest way to face anything life will throw at you.

The *wisdom share* in this chapter concerns helping you learn how to keep your soul reservoir pure and flowing by overcoming the challenges that life will present. Whenever you take an emotional deep-dive risk—such as venturing out of your comfort zone, attempting to learn something new or changing something that isn't working, or adding more to your plate—obstacles are almost inevitable. Life is full of twists, turns, blind spots, and so many questions. With the right soul chemistry, you will begin to make good decisions for yourself.

Your soul reservoir represents the navigation system (or self-value system) needed to make the right decision *for you*. Just as the sun will most likely come up in the east and set in the west tomorrow, an obstacle is most definitely on the horizon, bringing with it challenges and disappointments. Knowing yourself intimately and intricately, embracing a pure reservoir of belief and goodness about yourself will net you a more peaceful self-journey! You cannot prepare for something you don't know is coming, but you can prepare for what you do know and how you think when it does occur. That solid clear thinking is what comes from the condition of your soul.

So, what do the obstacles or "new holds" look like? Imagine yourself on a rock-climbing expedition. You are the lead climber. Your job is to find that next great hold and look beyond the fear of making that next leap. The new holds have certain characteristics and you'll sense those quickly. Most people believe an obstacle looks like more like a roadblock when it is more like a road map. The next hold may look impossible, but it is the answer to the next level up. Experienced climbers know good holds, and experienced life learners know that blocks and obstacles are on the road map to success. An obstacle we face is there because we may need to have a better plan, more clarity, and better decision-making. Perhaps we need a change in course. Obstacles come at you as problems, setbacks, but remember, they are the next hold.

When your soul reservoir is in harmony with your thought processes, you will navigate in and around any obstacle in life that presents itself. You may be faced with a split decision to choose which way you are going to go, either sinking into the depths of disparity and depression, or seizing the strength you have within you and becoming who you truly are meant to be. I choose how I feel about myself. Other people do not choose for me.

Chapter 8

Happiness Absolutely Comes from Within

W ithin our lifetime, we search for happiness externally through someone or something else. Let's look at some words and phrases that represent things we may believe bring us happiness.

Cuter
Thinner
More muscles
Nicer home
More luxurious car
Higher position
More clothes
More shoes
More things
More money
More time
Fewer wrinkles
Become older sooner (toddlers and teenagers)
Dating Sites
Glances at the stop light
Attention from the opposite sex
Indulgences
More perfect
Cars
Houses
Boats
Status

Better job
Higher Pay
Boyfriends
Girlfriends
Outside stimulation
Drugs
Sex
Work
Extramarital Affairs
Gambling
Drinking
Eating
Marriage
Buying more
Bigger
Better
Faster
Stronger

If we could only control our happiness through the things we obtain and people in our lives, we'd be just fine. Right? I'm here to tell you that's not the case. The reality is that we cannot control anything outside of our own body and our own thoughts. We feed our brains and our physical bodies what they need. What are you feeding yours? Let's take a simple example. This chair that I am sitting in right now could collapse completely, and within seconds I would be flat on my back. I am hoping that the structure of this chair will hold me, but I cannot control what will happen if the chair broke because I sat in it. What can I control? I can control how I sit in it, whether the weight is near the front or the back. I can control how big I get as far as food intake goes. And I can control my posture in the chair. Am I sitting upright, with my core engaged and my feet flat on the floor? I can only control the things I do or think.

Why is it that we believe we can obtain happiness through external items, people, or words? When you think about it, it is all just moving energy and perception; what we tell ourselves is far more important that what we hear and see from external sources. Everything outside of ourselves is an illusion of someone's imagination, yet we find ourselves asking, "Will that make me happy" or "This will bring me happiness" or "When this happens, I'll be really happy." Banking on *when* and *if* and *why not* is like banking on the chair holding me up if I gain 400 pounds. I know the weight capacity of the chair, but I'll sit in it anyway. You know that banking on other people's ideals or perceptions puts you in a world of hurt. Don't do it!

☼

So much happens around us at the speed of light! If you think for one minute you can control anything or anyone, you have another thing coming. The minute I gave up thinking I could control everything around me in terms of others' perception of me (and thinking theirs was more important than mine), I realized just how truly happy I was. Trying to control everything is like trying to pin down mercury. If you've ever played around with a broken thermometer, you know what I mean! If you controlled *everything*, you would become a slave to your controlled pieces in your life. That is no way to live. What will be, will be. We must let things go to be genuinely happy. This book is filled with wisdom for personal happiness and I am shouting it from the roof top: Let go of control. Let go of all the nonsense and bad chemistry in your soul reservoir and work hard not to take any more in.

Part of letting go of control is to stop controlling what people will think of you. I like newer cars because they give me less hassle. I've always liked to have a vehicle that is newer, clean, and worry-free, even though I know that they start depreciating the moment I sign the paperwork at the dealership. To some, cars are a status symbol and provide a way to control what people think of you. In our society, status can be found in the eye of the beholder, so a nice new car says, "I am somebody and I am successful." A crappy car might say to the onlookers, "I am poor and unsuccessful." Many people will decide how they feel about someone by the car they drive. So even our hologram takes on that responsibility to maintain a false imagery of ourselves for perhaps how others may feel about you. Maintaining a false sense of imagery or reality can be exhausting and harmful to your lasting healthy Hologram.

The same can be said for social media. Let's take Facebook. It's the equivalent of driving a "nice car." You think you can control what people think about you by what you post, respond to, or update. You think you can shape the opinion of others by words, pictures, and how often you respond. Does that social platform make you a good person, a good friend, or a great writer? Does what they think about you make a difference? Does having a ton of virtual friends make you a success?

Absolutely not. It can make you obsessive, trying to control others' reactions by sharing everything that you think may impress others and, in turn, make you happy. It's easy to think that your happiness is tied to having a lot of friends, and that you might be important, special, and ultimately be happy. That couldn't be any farther from the truth. We are delusional, once again if we think that outside circumstances will bring true happiness, it won't. Happiness comes from what you host in your soul, period.

56

What you host in your soul reservoir was absorbed from everyone and everything around you and NOW, you must determine if what you keep in your soul is necessary for lifelong happiness.

Your hologram, your true smile, your authentic happiness comes from being happy within yourself. You might be thinking, "Those are a bunch of words strung together, but what does that really mean in the whole scheme of things?" Happiness comes from within, but where is "within"? Your soul reservoir is where you host all your emotions and feelings. If you are hosting a ton of sadness, anger, frustration, and disappointment in your reservoir, your mind and body will continually pull from an unhappy reservoir. You'll not see the truth that you should embrace because it is diluted with false information and feelings. It is your job to purify, cleanse, wash, fix, and empty the reservoir of those unhappy emotions, by filling with positive, supportive and uplifting emotions. As the world evolves and becomes excessively overpopulated and emotionally diverse, it will be a greater challenge to ward off the intruding flow of complex negative and unhealthy emotions. But you can do it! Careful selection of whom you spend your time with and what you deposit into the emotional dispatch center is your choice. Happiness is an inside job and it starts with realizing your self-limiting beliefs that were adapted long before you found your own. Dive deep, find yourself, and live a happy life.

Chapter 9

Decision Making with a New Soul Reservoir

Life is a series of choices and decisions and those two actions are synonyms yet used extremely different in everyday life. Both actions use the soul reservoir as the foundational navigation system as the guide. Making decisions on how we feel about something may not always net us good results based on what our reservoir hosts. If you have garbage in, you might put garbage out. If you take in less than desirable messages you might make less than desirable actions for yourself. Hindsight is 20/20. I'm sure you've all heard that saying, or "If I knew then what I know now, things would be so different." Those are sayings we use when we've made a decision that didn't turn out so great. If you're filled with extremely low self-esteem, resentment and anger, your choices and decisions will not be healthy nor maybe accurate for you long term. Many times, if we are not fully aware of who we really are or what values we place before our decision-making upon, we will end up making decisions based on ill-gotten or false information. Perhaps we'll make choices that are completely opposite of how we really feel. We've all made decisions to second guess later.

How does our reservoir and soul diagram affect our decision-making overall? When we make a choice or decision, we begin to react physiologically and move with momentum in the direction. A decision, unlike a choice, is a complex process, and for many, it can be game-changing. A heftier decision might be, "Do I go to college right out of high school or take a year off?" A choice takes seconds to make, like, "breakfast or no breakfast?" That is why I feel that decision-making is critical to your overall personal happiness and choices are a whole lot less critical to happiness. Choices are based on the current moment, where decisions take some serious thinking and weighing out options. Sometimes quick choices are made because you feel cornered and just need to choose. It happens all the time. Mom says, "Pizza or macaroni?" And you choose pizza. Simple choice, but not life altering.

What if our decisions were based on information we were fed and still host, as opposed to what we know and *want to be true?* If you were raised to dislike white people and you knew it to be wrong, but made decisions based on that premise and going against how your soul reacts to that premise, would you make the necessary changes? Making decisions on what you were fed would leave you confused, and people do this all the time because somewhere, somehow along the way, the information they were given was false and tainted. We must try to not make decisions based on what someone else wants for us versus what we want. When we are young, we aren't strong enough to make decisions based on our own beliefs because we don't yet embrace our own belief and value system within ourselves. We attempt to base decisions upon psychological history, condition of our soul, current information, outside pressure or control factors, cognitive abilities at the time, possible outcomes or benefits most applicable to the immediate situation, as well as white noise from an assortment of stimuli outside of our control. A choice might be as simple as which blouse to wear. The red blouse or the white one? Or, "Do I want pork or beef for dinner?" Sometimes, decisions that alter the course of your life are made way before you even had a say in anything, i.e., your religion, the role you play in your family, what you like or dislike, whether you are racist, hateful, vengeful, healthy, unhealthy, and so many more things. Whether or not your mom chose to feed you an apple or an orange on any given day won't alter your life too much. Decisions, on the other hand, based on someone else's value systems, will alter who you are forever. Get to know your value systems.

I have a solid history of making good decisions that allow me to experience a strong selection of what life has to offer. My decisions were based upon my drive, desires, and what I knew I knew I wanted. Were they easy to make? Not so much. I was riddled with confusion and had an adopted scarcity mentality that kept me failing time after time. I'd reach great heights only to pull the pin on obtaining my goals. The condition of the soul factors into the decision-making process so much so, that without the soul, a decision would be completely void of who you are – even though you are making decisions before the soul isn't completely comprised 100% of your chemistry. It makes no sense to leave your soul out of the decision-making process. Your soul is that gut feeling derived from years of your emotions or that of someone else. Going forward, always make sure your soul is in balance and harmony with who you know you are today. Don't decide based on what someone else thinks you should do, ever. When you leave your soul influence out of the mix, for whatever reason—choosing not to cleanse the soul or check in with it prior to a major decision—chances are that you will look back and realize it wasn't the best decision for YOU. It might be the best decision for someone else. The key to solid personal decision-making is to have a pure reservoir and a pure you.

Can choices affect decisions, and vice versa? The answer is yes. Will one of them become easier to do if you make better choices for yourself? It should. Whether or not you eat pork or beef for dinner won't ultimately make that big of a difference. The decision to never eat meat again could ultimately affect your life, long-term. Is one more important than the other? That answer is, it depends. I've lived in Wisconsin and Minnesota. Asking myself whether I should wear some socks today is, at times, an important decision. If I decide to forego socks, there is a good chance that my feet will be cold all day, never warm up, and stay cold right up to bedtime. A choice to wear red, white, or black socks is incidental, depending on my initial *decision to* wear socks. After many months, many years of living in a cold climate, the decision to wear wool socks can make or break an entire outing or day. Depending on the temperature, the thickness of the wool is another decision I make before heading out of the house.

Decisions are complex, whereas choices are simpler undertakings, born of answering an immediate need. Are you beginning to see the difference? So, when you hear, "Life is a series of choices," it's true, but those choices are less complicated than decisions. We can all make smarter choices and decisions going forward! Some choices and some decisions are made for you way too early, but your life doesn't stop there. Creating your own soul reservoir based on who you are and what you know to be true will make all the difference.

What comes first, the choice or the decision? I believe that choice comes first. "Would you like a peas or carrots for supper?" We begin making choices long before we can decide. We are given a choice and then as we begin to gain knowledge and experience and make decisions based on facts or actual life experiences of our own, or from a reservoir that serves us. Sadly, some of us are born into an environment where all our choices are made by the people around us, and there isn't anything we can do about it until we are wise and strong enough to make new and better choices for ourselves. Life begins with a pure reservoir. The luck of the draw for many at an early age can be so harsh and even unreal. Many people end up in such cruel situations, yet come out the other side triumphantly and with renewed purpose and strength. Nothing can take away the fire in your belly because that fire is the soul. We all have one. The sooner you realize that you have choices and can make better decisions—even when others are making them for you or only revealing part of the picture—the better everything will become, the more pure your hologram will be, and the less likely you will be to end up unhappy.

To me, happiness comes from knowing who you are and becoming the person you want to become. The only way to truly know yourself is through trial and error, and learning from choices and decisions you make all on your own. So, a simple question. Do you want an apple pie or a hot fudge sundae for dessert? I'll leave that choice up to you. Do YOU like hot fudge better than the apple pie? Do you know? Would you know if put to the test? This book is about getting to know who YOU are, what YOU want and like and most importantly, loving yourself without any input or conditions from others.

Chapter 10

Never Entitled to Affect Others Negatively

Happiness comes from knowing who you are and becoming the person you want to become, so the hard work of getting personal with your soul reservoir can pay off for you and everyone around you. When applied consistently, discipline in any area of life will net a good or bad outcome. Neglect is a form of discipline. Neglecting to take care of yourself continuously is a form of discipline. Disciplining yourself to not overeat can be a monumental undertaking and so rewarding if you are trying to be healthy or lose weight. A lot of us will not admit we eat too much because then we have to do something about it. Still, most overweight or troubled individuals spend many hours a day doing the one thing that keeps them so unhappy! Some will even say over and over to feel a sense of justification: "Well, obesity runs in my family." I call bullshit on that statement. But because some people have disciplined their mind in a negative fashion to accept the obesity gene and curse, the outcome for them remains obesity.

Discipline can also work in your favor if you institute positive work towards happiness and self-love. Understanding why you do the things you do would be a great start, wouldn't it? Why do I eat way beyond what I need? Am I eating for emotional reasons? This applies to everything we do and continue to do where the outcome really starts to dominate our health. Maybe it's drinking too much alcohol, creating a life of alcoholism. Maybe by overeating or drinking too much is now the way you say to yourself, I'm not enough or worthy.

It's a mistake to believe that we are entitled to a certain belief system that was never ours to begin with. I often hear, "Well, my mom did it that way," or "My dad showed me this." Just because we were shown something doesn't necessarily mean we are entitled to continue with that behavior or belief system. Not everything we were taught or heard is healthy to believe or act on. We are never entitled to any behavior, especially using negative feelings for continued self-abuse or abuse of others. That organically instilled chemistry in your soul reservoir may create a mentality of entitlement which becomes the downfall of yourself, your family, foundations, and ultimately, our society. If we were given a role model who abused their spouse, we need to put up a block against that behavior immediately. If we were shown racism, we shouldn't perpetuate that feeling or thought process. Many people do not do the work to become a healthier, happy individual. Instead, they slide into a place of self- apathy. We are not entitled to continue a self-deprecating behavior because someone showed us or dealt with us in a less-than-ideal hand. No excuses. Everyone deserves to understand why they do what they do and to have a chance to get it right. You learned your behavior somewhere along the way. If you are mean to an animal, it is completely unacceptable. You'd better get your act together and figure out what makes you so angry that you would take it out on an innocent animal! Don't perpetuate the idiocy or the soul diagram given to you by someone else who is unsuspecting of their own hurts and chemistry.

Considering yourself special, entitled, or requiring compliance from a system or others, will net you disappointment and will fill your soul with negative chemistry. The world will reject that notion in every capacity, every time. You may find yourself in an emotional state that cannot be soothed. To feel better, you'll go looking for automatic compliance—a safe place where you feel the same before self-cleansing—and become more and more disheartened. You grew up in chaos, so continuing chaos feels "right" to you. It is a thought process and chemistry that needs to change to find personal happiness and have a hologram consistent with inner peace and self-love. Once you've finally eliminated entitlement from your bag of tricks, you can never reinstate it! Making excuses or believing you are entitled to carry on the chemistry from someone who was unhealthy emotionally will only continue the cycle of distress for you and those you encounter. Do not accept a tainted soul. You don't have to, so let it go. It's not yours.

To have personal happiness, a great place to start is recognizing that an entitlement mentality will only add deception and greed to your reservoir. Entitlement or perpetuating bad behaviors without change is a recipe for disaster. To keep your eyes on the prize (ongoing lifelong happiness), learn when entitlement is directing your steps. You don't have to be an alcoholic just because your mom or dad took that path.

How do you know if your behaviors and decisions come from a healthy or unhealthy place? Your first clue will most likely be an overall sadness, coming from a frustrated and incongruent soul. Before you enter any type of relationship think long and hard about this chapter of entitlement and the work your soul needs to breathe and feel happy. I don't blame anyone for what my life is or isn't. But I will blame myself when I leave my soul reservoir in a condition that is less than I know it can be. The only thing you are entitled to, is true unadulterated happiness. Go get it!

Chapter 11

Know Love

As you keep your soul reservoir clean and pure from anything that will take away from your happiness, you will want to experience something more: love. The feeling of love is indescribable, but I am going to try to explain it the best way I know how to, so that you can reach for that brass ring and feel the self-love and love for others that you deserve. Love is there and everyone deserves love. The young, old, helpless, homeless, disabled, maimed, imprisoned, psychotic, forgotten, addicted, left to die, happy, fake, living the dream, short, tall, fat, skinny, fearful, feared, cute, not-so-cute, homely, ugly, unhappy, cute, beautiful, depressed, angry, furry four-legged, furry two-legged, sinners and saints. I've loved someone in every one of these categories and each felt the same because love cannot discriminate. The same goes for self-love, because once you do the work on your soul reservoir, asking all those hard questions, you will no longer discriminate against yourself or others.

Love can only come from an unhardened and cleansed soul. And an unhardened soul comes from a place of understanding and forgiveness for others, and itself. As crazy as it may sound, some people are afraid of love. They will take almost every other emotion you have to offer them, but love is the one thing they will refuse. They don't love themselves.

The hologram of your soul cannot be complete without loving yourself, allowing yourself to be loved, and to love unconditionally. That authentic smile on your face arrives only after you have experienced all of those and continue to experience them on a regular basis. As I write this, huge tears are streaming down my face. No one should ever feel unloved, but a high percentage of people walk around on this planet feeling unloved. Many don't love themselves. How truly awful is that?

What is love? Love is sacrifice, conviction, and acceptance. To love and receive love, we need all three. God so loved his children that he gave his only son—sacrifice, conviction and acceptance of the greatest magnitude. The men and women who sign up to go to war have those three characteristics. Parents who will do anything and forgive anything for their children, experience love beyond most. Love takes on many forms, but each time it is given is beautiful.

Yet, why is it so hard to give and to receive love? Ask yourself how much you are willing to sacrifice, how strong your convictions are. Can you accept and give unconditional love? Some may never choose to love again after one time around, while others will dive right in again. Some were hurt so deeply in their youth that self-love and love of others seems unreachable. They were hurt at some point and the memory of the hurt took away their ability to sacrifice. Their conviction is so strong now, but in the opposite direction of love that it will be almost impossible to return to even a neutral place. They have built walls of protection versus swells of love. They live a life of cat and mouse. *I give this to you, so you will give this to me. They never fully invest into the true ability to love.* It is out of obligation and fear of being alone that they give and take, always staying one step ahead so someone always owes them something. That isn't love. That's *gambling,* and they get rather good at it!

The Hologram of the Soul is about love and happiness extruding from every pore in your being and the smile that will light up on your face. For me, love is a constitution, and it would go against my hologram if I didn't feel it, act it, share it, and own it. My mom once told me that I needed to turn the other cheek. I asked her why, and what for, because (I said) both of my cheeks were the same, love. What I meant was that I would love no matter what, even when the wrath of someone else is deflecting onto me. I don't understand how love can't be in the equation when it comes to human interaction. People shy away from love for all kinds of reasons. It is sad. You must be able to love yourself through conviction, sacrifice, and acceptance. Whether it is how you take care of yourself, or a steadfast loyalty to a friend, or loyalty to a cause. The cause may be your family. Love yourself better than you love others, so that you can love others just as much as you love yourself.

Chapter 12

Perfect Life List

For years, I've carried a list of how my perfect life would be when I "get there," and I tweak it occasionally to refine the list, so it resonates with how my perfect life would be based on my thoughts and reservoir decisions. My list is a work in progress and sometimes it can change, but it's still pretty much in concrete and I try not to waver much. This list is a depiction of all the things that I value and want so I could have that joy that comes from my own ideas of my perfect life and not what someone else deems to be my perfect life list. My list has things on it like good friends—more of them and closer in proximity so they can stop by, stay over, or have coffee. The perfect list really should be a strategic plan to keep what is going well and working in your life and keep out what isn't nor was ever yours to begin with. All the while, continually adding more to your list that aligns with your soul. What makes me happiest of all is helping others via speaking, coaching, or writing. When I am doing those activities, I am in heaven, on earth.

The Hologram of the Soul is that authentic, amazing, bright, unadulterated and brilliant smile, that deep, beautiful essence that permeates through every pore of your being. That smile begins and stays with you when you make a commitment to understand who you really are and who you love without conditions. You see, the list of my perfect life is a list of commitments that I need to make to myself and to others, only achieved once I fully love myself. Even if at some point our life the list is shattered—if our dreams taken away, the course of events changed, immediate decisions trump current events, the floor is blown away out from under us—the list, *my very important list*, still exists. Those written beliefs, values, and dreams of mine didn't die. The road to get there may have ended, but the list of my perfect life did not.

When your belief system is shaped too early, rattled or broken because of something outside of your control, or the list gets completely gutted, there will come a moment when you let go of the before list because it's not relevant or doable any longer. A new list will emerge, a list that is more congruent with your soul today. Many of my girlfriends have experienced divorce, some from a cheating spouse, and as devastating as that is, they've come out from under the clouds carrying the very personal list of their perfect life in their heads and hearts. We all have them; we just don't call them our "perfect life" list, but instead, dreams, hopes, wishes, fantasies, or whatever you deem them to be. We craft our life by making sure we have this list of our perfect life after we go through hell. I say, figure out now who you are and create the list. Don't waste as much time or effort as I parse my soul to everyone else but me.

The purpose of the subtitle (Wisdom for Personal Happiness), is to share tips about how to get that authentic smile on your face. I believe that if you take care of your soul it will reflect on your face. And keeping that list of your perfect life current, sharp, and detailed is a part of the entire Hologram of the Soul process. I am in the process of recreating my perfect life list for the 5th or 6th time in my life bases on decisions I have made.

People may resent that you're working towards authenticity, and your list, because the life they are living is full of outcomes from bad mistakes or impulse decisions. They aren't enjoying what they have created. If you are happy with your life, people with tainted or unresolved reservoirs will gravitate towards you to clip you off at the knees. Those people are miserable and would just as soon have you be miserable right along with them! We've all met them, and their life is full of "have to" and not "want to". Due to obligation and necessity, their lives cannot change, they just can't become the person they desire to be. Maybe more like you. Many times, their continued unhappiness and angst is due to demands from their unplanned—or ill-planned—life that places tremendous, unwanted responsibility on them. It might be due to mental illness, neglect of their social group or their own body that looms over them like a dark cloud on a rainy day. A lack of soul-tending, and missing their "perfect life list," has pretty much ruined their life. In turn, they will try to ruin yours, or at least make you miserable. There's a trade-off with everything and a price to pay for staying in something you don't want, something that denies your personal and emotional freedom. Your list will help you determine the path you choose to reach a destiny of unconditional love and personal happiness. And by destiny, I mean the emotionally healthy, happy, and fulfilled hologram of the soul.

Can destinations change due to unforeseen circumstances? Yes. I wish they didn't, but they do, and for all the right and wrong reasons. We see ourselves on one path and,

70

low and behold, we are off on another path for some odd reason or circumstance. Life, jobs, families, health, and financial situations can throw a big monkey-wrench into our "perfect life list," and we have to take the time to breathe, back off of the list, and realize we must now pause and focus to handle what has just taken place. "How did I get so off track, or on another track altogether, and why do I feel so disjointed?" There are too many things out of our control, but there are so many more that *are* within our control.

For example: start by picking the right people to be in your life. Can you imagine the difference in our life had we had a choice in the people we picked to be in our lives or as a mate? You should be picking quality people with the new pure soul reservoir you will have!

The following questions will help you build your list according to your happiness. Even if you believe in your heart that your life can never be the way you want it again, hold on to a new belief that more happiness is just around the corner, because it is.

Do I want what I have and feel how I feel *for myself,* or for someone else?

Have I had what I am experiencing now before, and does it serve me well, or was it given to me?

Is this going to add to my authenticity and hologram, or will it make me unhappy?

Why am I doing what I am doing right now?

These are some difficult questions to ask yourself as you make the perfect life list, but nonetheless, questions that will ultimately help you find your values and beliefs. Your values and beliefs are really the only ones that will matter along the way and in the end. So, ask yourself, is what I want on my perfect life list in line with my beliefs and values? Ask until you can't ask the question anymore.

Another example of an unauthentic soul diagram or life list is putting others wants and needs before your own. I believe everyone has the capacity to think about the other guy in terms of wanting to do something nice for them or add to their life. The problem is, when we are emotionally neglected as a child, we tend to emotionally neglect ourselves along the way in our own lives. We continue to be an emotional burden to our personal progress and ultimately our bigger life picture as well. Placing others needs before your own or being a people-pleaser can result in a life of endless supposed friends and heartache never really getting what you need. We are seeking from others their perceived value of us and what they think, do, and believe to be okay about us. They have complete power over our own thoughts of self. This book is about thriving and performing at your absolute best, making life choices within split seconds ("in an instant" Remember chapter one!) for yourself based on your beliefs. Being able to make choices and decisions successfully within seconds takes a solid understanding of the goodness inside of you. With your perfect life list based on what you want and need, the choices and decisions will be a whole lot easier to make. When it comes to "the perfect life list," think in these terms: Will the things I add to my list bring me to an emotional state where I will thrive in happiness and health? If the answer is a resounding yes, add it! Create the perfect life list and remember, because someone else has or had a crappy life list doesn't mean you have to take on their life list or emotional intelligence.

Chapter 13

Soul Canvas

In chapter four, I talk about the clean reservoir, writing:
"Go on a hunt. Become the predator, finding all lingering negative chemistry, gathering it up and replacing it with brand new chemistry. Find positive emotions gleaned from positive experiences that dispel and replace any negative emotions. Start a new mantra with specific words / emotions that you want: purity, peace, calm, normalcy, integrity, and morality."

We addressed the "perfect life list" in Chapter 12. I referred to your "soul canvas" in chapter four, but in this chapter, 13, I want to really expound on what your soul canvas is, and how to achieve what's best for yours.

A canvas is a visual that results from data turned into a graphic. What we put in emotional dispatch then travels into our soul reservoir, which will, in time, create an image. And that image will reflect on our face. The one thing everyone can see, and that society puts so much emphasis on, is the human face. We are now down to a 1 x 1 picture of our face plastered everywhere from social media to email to our phone. The one identity—the canvas created from years of absorption of internal dialogue and external contribution—is who you are. Is the face a true canvas of your happiness or unhappiness? I believe that the face is a depiction of how you feel emotionally, and it draws the canvas from the chemistry in your soul reservoir. The Hologram will take the message from the canvas derivatives and illuminate your face in right fashion with its directives. As you read this book, how are you truly feeling inside? What messages keep going through your head? Are they uplifting, happy feelings and thoughts, or are they the opposite? Are you feeling positive or negative? I have continuous negative tapes that I must squelch, or my life would literally be miserable. I could drink alcohol and lift my spirits, but I just can't handle the hangover anymore. Some people have to drink to stay up. Alcoholism is a wicked disease.

Holograms are everywhere. Just look at people in the face and feel who they are. In some gruesome murder cases, the murderer smiles upon hearing the verdict. That smile can only come from one place. I believe that smile comes from their soul, their personal constitution and belief system, and feeling of justification that what they did was awesome. Over time, the input became the reality and the face became the display. When a murder smiles upon hearing the guilty verdict, that smile comes from chemistry that supports the notion that he was justified in committing murder. That is how powerful soul chemistry is. We must guard what we absorb and host.

The Soul Canvas is the one thing you can help along the way by inputting the things to make the hologram that much more beautiful. Things like positive people, healthy people with healthy goals, spirituality, your God, dreams, and positive activities. Surround yourself with people who have worked on getting their soul reservoir cleansed and practice keeping it pure, so that they will spread health, kindness, and fairness. Surround yourself with those who emit happiness. In a perfect world, this is what I see as one way to make a big impact on your hologram and that of others. The soul canvas is what you will show the outside world.

I have done volunteer work with those that are recovering from addiction and those that are in some of the darkest places of their lives. On their road back, as they are absorbing and believing better information into emotional dispatch and into their reservoir, their face begins to change and glow. A smile appears and you can see the joy inside of their soul radiating on their face. They cannot deny it. Neither will you as your new canvas begins to emerge in full color and light! Those innocent but drug-addicted teenagers are no longer held captive by drugs, and they begin to like themselves again. The work, however, isn't just to stop ingesting drugs, it is when one looks at their soul and faces each emotion.

Once you realize you are creating that soul canvas, the input choices and decisions you make will work a lot more to your advantage. Someone once said to me, "You look a lot younger when you smile." I think there is some truth to that. When you lie to yourself and others your soul takes on an instant negative chemistry, almost impossible to hide in your face. Adding negative things into your chemistry mix is just as bad as lying. Since we are all works in progress, don't you think we should start cleansing the reservoir right away?

Regardless of when we start, we will encounter others with reservoirs so tainted with mega amounts of lifelong held captive impurities. You know how you feel today regarding certain emotions you carry with you. It's no different when you are someone that emits a negative flow of energy. It's almost indescribable, but we feel it. We might even say something like, "It just didn't feel right." When dating, a lot of people will refer to that feeling as "chemistry." I believe there is a "chemistry" within each of us that emits energy to others and into the world. In almost every human interaction, we are jockeying for spiritual positioning within our own soul and the souls of those we meet. Detecting the negative information immediately and by not allowing it into emotional dispatch we will decrease the amount of work later. And ultimately, our canvas that we've worked very hard at creating will reflect the happiness we so deserve. Anything outside of your own personal truth and conviction will have no chance of ever polluting our most amazing clean and content reservoir. The reservoir within our soul system is the foundation of personal happiness.

Chapter 14

Pain and our Reservoir, No More Pain. Happy Chapter!

Let's address the subject of unresolved emotional pain. I know writing "about pain" as an opening line can seem like a doom and gloom subject, but without it we cannot reach a place of emotional freedom. While pain seems to be inevitable in life, it doesn't have to be your life story. If you are experiencing lagging, long overdue unresolved emotional pain in your life, then this chapter is designed to address that concern. Pain is something that we can, quite frankly, diminish or abolish once we choose to find the source of the pain. Just as physical pain can be real and healed, emotional pain can as well. We can regulate or abolish unresolved emotional pain.

Does our mind know the difference between physical and emotional pain? When does emotional pain begin and when does it end? Is this a bad subject to address? Will I bring us to a place where we'd rather not go emotionally? Will you go there? By now, I am hoping we can agree upon the fact that pain from unresolved emotional issues is real. I promise that the journey through this chapter will elevate your knowledge and comfort level surrounding the idea of unresolved emotional pain and take you to a place where you will find beauty, freedom, and peace.

Emotional pain can most certainly precede physical pain, but it isn't so readily noticeable nor detected until it emerges or manifests later in life. It might take years before the unresolved pain in the soul will affect the physical wellbeing. People with depression know this all too well. Depression hurts. This is a saying often used in by the media to sell antidepressants to those struggling with depression. Depression does cause physical pain in the human body and comes from years of neglect or negative oppressive thoughts that were handed to us on a silver platter. Over time, little by little, because we are unaware, our reservoir is left stagnant with all the emotions from unresolved unattended soul reservoir bad stinky chemistry. Many forms of autoimmune diseases began their journey in the reservoir and left to fester through years of suppression and depression. In efforts to be happy and free, we must dive into the stink and clear it out!

Why do we have depression and do we all experience depression in some form in our life. The answer is a resounding yes! When I think of depression, I envision a huge thumb putting pressure on a piece of silly putty, creating a deep large imprint. I also picture a mechanical car-crusher annihilating an old rusty car for scrap. Emotional depression is the unrelenting, repetitious pressure from repeating messages of self-sabotaging suppressed emotions in our soul. Believing the imprint of what others have determined you to be or become. Something so far from your truth and how you should live. Depression has its foothold in suppression and is the root cause in miscommunication, misunderstandings, and hurt in all types of relationships including those within childhood. I believe we cease to exist, and happiness evades us when we carry and repeat the bad chemistry emotions that we inherited. I strongly believe that we absorb and host the energy from those around us, whether it be good or bad. Stay around emotionally, mentally, and physically healthy people and you will feel lifted, infused with energy, and inspired. Spend time around unhealthy people and you will become unhealthy. As an adult you can choose who you give soul real estate to.

We are not here to devour each other for the sake of our own existence yet people with unattended depressed or unhealthy polluted soul reservoirs do just that. In fact, they only know that way. Control and manipulation are their go-to activities. In the animal kingdom, predators kill to survive. Humans use guilt, manipulation, judgement, control, and abuse to offset personal ignorance or denial. If you choose to bring children into this world to coexist with other humans, you must choose to become an emotionally healthy human. Do the work and feel the reward of physiological calm. Just using cognitive abilities to impact the growth of a child isn't even remotely enough to prepare a child for the world. As adults we must bring continuous authentic nurturing to a child that is absorbing their emotional health from everyone they encounter. As adults we must become aware of our own emotional health and make the effort to love ourselves before another human life is impacted. We must decide to become emotionally happy so we can become the fully functioning happy adults that we need to be to live full and happy lives. The realization begins the minute we begin to fix our emotional health for self-preservation and the preservation of human life, so the negative imprint is lessoned or null and void.

We affect one another greatly and whether the energy is spoken or not, the energy and chemistry is landing in emotional dispatch. As children we are unable to notice the idiosyncrasies of the bad energy, but we absorb it all like a sponge. Children take in everything they feel, and it can be positive, negative, or very hurtful.

Unfortunately, we are not able to read the minds of others, so we are not able to control their words or actions. But we can feel their energy, can't we? We also can only control our own thoughts. For extremely sensitive empaths like myself, we act and react upon our hosted emotional chemistries and anyone who might be in our energy field. I also react to the fear feelings when I am around others who live a "fear life." The other emotional chemistry that I picked up along the way was the doubt emotion. The doubt gene or feeling that was inserted along the way was not something I chose. Children so easily can pick up the doubt gene or chemistry from their immediate influence and not understand how to deal with what they feel at that time. Children accept what others say or defer to others because children do not have the skill or brain circuitry at such a young age to combat what is being felt. Empaths—and I believe that we all have sensitivities like empaths—are highly intuitive and complete feelers. Feelings are very real, whereas with words may land in emotional dispatch but feelings carry chemistry that travel to our soul reservoir. I would rather feel chemistry and know myself and others by their chemistry then by words or even actions at times. Detecting good chemistry is by far, *much more REAL*. Knowing your emotional chemistry will give you a greater understanding of yourself and others when you are in their presence. Remember the saying, "People will forget what you say, but never forget how you make them feel." Absolute truth! So, bottom line, if you are self-abusing or abusing others, you have the job of fixing yourself before you impact someone else. The excuse of "I didn't know," or, "They did the best they could," isn't enough and cannot be perpetuated any longer. "Stop the insanity" was also a great saying somewhere along the way.

We are addressing the pain in our life that is kept afloat in our soul reservoir. Since we cannot control the soul reservoir of another human, we can control what goes in our emotional dispatch and stays in our soul reservoir. So, controlling emotional pain is completely doable. So, take a moment to feel beautiful feelings and watch how easy it is to breathe for a moment in time? Seriously, stop for a bit, feel incredible feelings of love and happiness and feel how you breathe. Stand alongside a river, lake or ocean, listening to the water and waves. The energy from the water puts us in a state of mind that is calming and tranquil. Might feel like all the worries have washed away. What is magnificent about taking in calm and beautiful surroundings is for that moment, you are without pain, and when you are doing something you absolutely enjoy, you are without pain. Your emotional health is engaged into something you love to do! The level at which our emotional health appears, and functions is available within our own grasp within "an instant." One or many feelings of good or bad will create emotional chemistry. If you choose a life of happiness and a life without pain, work on your emotional health!

When I'm petting a dog, I do not feel any pain. None. I feel only unconditional love for the dog and the dog feels unconditional love for me. I've heard story after story of how, when people are doing something they absolutely love, they feel no pain in their physical body. Grandparents who are with their grandchildren experience nothing but joy, hunters in a tree stand for hours at an end feel nothing but "one" with the woods. I've read stories about surgeons who are in the deepest part in a surgery, experiencing ecstasy because they are accomplishing something so amazing. Some liken it to an out-of-body experience. Women quilting together, doing something physical with their hands, are in such a place of contentedness that their illnesses, aches, and pains subside for the duration of their time together. Story after story, person after person... People do find a life without pain. When I write, I can feel the pain in my elbows and neck, but when I am deep within the writing process, I do not notice the pain. It is possible then, that when our emotional dispatch is clear and soul are in the right place, our physical body follows. Healing begins and some have healed absolute physical ailments to extraordinary measures.

Do you believe what I have written in the paragraphs above? If not, I feel strongly that you need to give it a try. Time to do an exercise. Put on a beautiful piece of music. Soft spa music, ocean waves, or the sound of a babbling brook. First read this, then read it again, then, put a place holder at this page. Here is your exercise and repeat as needed:

Close your eyes. Breathe normally for one minute, counting each breath. Don't worry about when the minute is up, just keep breathing. Keeping your eyes closed, without forcing them to stay shut, and complete this sentence: "All the positive energy in the world will find me and fill me for all the days of my life." Keep repeating this until you are completely relaxed and in harmony with your breathing. We can do this for as long as we need to fill our soul with as much positive energy as possible. We can never have enough of the good stuff. This should become a daily regular exercise. Repeat as needed.

Mental or physical pain is something that can be monitored and controlled. Emotional pain is different. We don't have to invite pain into our soul; we can manage our intake once we know we can accept, hold, or eliminate the pain from our emotional dispatch. The emotional dispatch is where we begin the process of the Hologram of the Soul. The reservoir holds the chemistry of good or negative chemistries that will scribe the EFFECT on our face. Remember, ultimately, we are in complete control of our emotional health. And my belief is that our emotional health controls, monitors, regulates our physical well-being all the days of our lives.

Chapter 15

Feeding the Soul

In this chapter, instead of specifically going over a list of words, feelings, and chemistries that we should or should not allow into emotional dispatch, or put into anyone else's, I would like to address the feelings that come from absorbing words or emotions at a time when we are unaware and emotionally ill-prepared to manage our soul reservoir chemistry. This book is about learning we have a reservoir—a holding tank, so to speak—and how to maintain the reservoir for perfect harmony and balance. The book is also designed to enlighten our knowledge that we all at some point are involved in filling someone else's reservoir, hopefully in a positive healthy way. Our job is twofold, making sure our own reservoir is healthy, and making sure that we won't taint that of another human by deflecting our inefficiencies onto them.

Prior to the actual cognitive awareness of our environment, the players in our life are busy at work, making lasting impressions and influencing our emotional state or self-esteem. Unfortunately, this is when most of the neurological and psychological magic, or destruction, happens. Absorption of others' chemistry (emotional wounds or health) happens before we can defend our emotional and psychological well-being. We just are major receptors—sponges absorbing every word, feeling, and every environmental impression. It happens when we are children, ages 0-18, and sometimes beyond.

As children, we learn our emotional neurology and direct or indirect responses from our earliest environmental factors, stimulants, depressors, or influences encompassing the positive, negative, and everything in between. Because we may be "in the line of fire" of a damaged or misguided person, when we absorb sights, words, and feelings the long-term effects can do us mental, emotional, and physical harm, leading to a life filled with poor decisions and low self-esteem. Or maybe the opposite is true. You have an unbelievably extraordinary and happy life. The "soup," our soul reservoir, can turn out good or bad; it all depends on what was thrown into the pot at the beginning of the soup-making process. Sometimes Oregano or Cilantro just isn't the right herb.

Ultimately, this book is about overcoming low self-esteem, self-abusive, neglectful behaviors, and irrational emotional processing, At the same time, I'd like to influence new generations to take care of the "self" prior to exposing themselves onto new life, i.e., procreating and making more humans. It's important to break the cycle, never repeating what someone did to you along the way. Some of us are more curious than others as to why we think, act, and feel or don't feel. Living in denial that you are feeling a certain way only perpetuates unhappiness and self-abuse.

I questioned many things at the tender age of eighteen. Before the start of my college freshman year, I made an appointment to see a psychiatrist. I wanted to talk about the way I felt inside. I wanted to know if how I was feeling was justified, given all my environments and happenings as a child, or inherited in some other way. That decision to talk about my feeling taught me so much, changing my life, and launching me on the road to introspection and expression of self, was so necessary to a life of self-love. It began my journey to understand myself emotionally.

I recommend therapy, counseling, or psychological assistance as much as you feel you need. I've sought some sort of therapy for most of my adult life, even during specific traumatic times. Keep looking until you find someone you can talk to freely about your feelings and belief systems. Many of my therapists would tell me that they just enjoyed having me because I was in tune with my feelings, and *they learned from me*. Understanding feelings and being able to express them in a non-biased nonjudgmental environment and way begins the healing process. No matter what has happened to you in your childhood or in adulthood, cleansing the soul reservoir is necessary so you can begin feeding the soul healthy thought patterns, beliefs, feelings and emotions.

Humankind, I am convinced, isn't always aware that their reservoir has taken in a new chemistry. So, their words, actions, lack of nurturing, or own baggage will affect others by virtue of this new chemistry being hosted and refed to themselves and others. If parents, teachers, adults, etc., aren't aware of their own behaviors, feelings, emotions, or self-abusive tendencies, while it may not interrupt their personal life plan or goals, the people around them can suffer greatly. Furthermore, if a child needs more nurturing and the parents or system does not have it to give, the child will always feel unworthy, invisible, or forgotten.

Emotional hurt can come in all forms throughout life. If we are unaware that our opinion of ourselves matters more than someone else's, we will walk around with *their* opinions launching every thought and action, until we fix it. For a child, it can be extremely hard to differentiate opinions and belief systems. Children believe everything around them and everything in a child's environment affects the outcome of that child's perception of self-worth. Every emotional feeling you absorb, positive or negative—all the words, the lack of nurturing or attention, the physical and emotional abuse, the name-calling, lack of validation or approval by manipulation or discount—every single thing that happens in a household, classroom, church, or in the public will shape a child's self-esteem and beliefs. Once out of the nest, each child must navigate life within the framework of the messages and soul reservoir developed in childhood, pricing to be a true disadvantage. It's like throwing paint against a canvas and hoping something positive or amazing will appear. You never quite know the outcome.

The important work on yourself begins when you leave the nest or societal influence and begin to believe your own experiences, apart from everything you learned growing up. You must understand why you feel, think, and act the way you do or the cycle of self-sabotage, sense of low self-esteem, narcissistic tendencies, or perfectionism will continue to emerge and dominate your life. I've never coached or met a person who doesn't have a reservoir created by all the years spent within the system that raised them.

To understand how things are shaped for a child from early on, let's consider the feelings of guilt. Everyone seems to understand or at least have felt guilt somewhere along the way.

Because guilt is widespread and very consuming, it becomes like a damp suffocating blanket in which we wrap ourselves, a default guidance system. While masked as other feelings, it can play out in horrible decision-making. Remember, guilt is one chemical in our reservoir, one of many amongst the mix of positive and negative emotions in our soul reservoir. After a while, guilt makes a nice cozy warm home within our reservoir, and we carry this emotional negative response system, or blanket, as a reminder to perpetuate and use for every decision and response.

Do we come out of the womb with feelings of guilt? NO. We come into this world with a clean slate, mind, body, and soul, thus, a clean emotional reservoir. The feeling of guilt that we gleaned as a child might have been a communication tactic by an authority figure, sometimes religious, within the family or through the education system as a tool or manipulation. "Why would you want to hurt mommy like that?" Does a three-year-old really understand their actions? Would they deliberately decide to hurt mommy? Of course not, but a child *feels* the message of guilt, absorbing it and acting from it until they realize it's in there and they need to shed the guilt. Feelings and emotions can run deeper than any other chemistry within our mind, body, and soul. We readily can forget words... but *feelings* are embedded for life, even if the person responsible has no idea what they've just done.

Does having guilt serve us in any positive and helpful way? To me, making decisions without guilt are far more beneficial than those decisions made with guilt in the mix. Guilt is a learned emotion, a negative that can be used as a tool to manipulate others into believing, thinking, feeling, and acting. If guilt was used throughout your childhood, it may be a part of your soul reservoir, and quite possibly is one of your "go to" emotions.

When is guilt a healthy activity? Guilt usually is something we feel after the fact.

According to the Cambridge Dictionary, second edition, guilt is:
"a feeling of anxiety or unhappiness that you have done something immoral or wrong, such as causing harm to another person."

People within our circle of influence use guilt as a corrective tool or to prevent certain behaviors. It's not healthy to live your live, driven by the emotion of guilt.

If you suffer with low self-esteem, your guilt-ridden reservoir guides you in decisions, determining relationship status and even your lifelong career. You may be unknowingly using guilt to control or manipulate someone you love, as this is part of who; it feels so natural. If you are a parent or a teacher and a child has blurted out, "Stop *guilting* me into this," that's a strong indication that you're using guilt as a tool on others.

We all can carry a form of guilt into daily situations. You try to be happy, taking a step forward for yourself, but guilt comes right along for that ride. My therapist once said, "Where you go, you will follow." It is so true. Until you stop, ask the right questions, face the negative emotion riding along with you, you'll continue to carry a tool bag that includes manipulating others with guilt. While guilt may seem familiar and comfortable, using guilt on yourself or others will never serve you, or them, in a healthy way.

Not all people are wise enough to stop the cycle of self-abuse or abuse on others. This takes the work being very self-aware, never allowing a negative emotion into emotional dispatch or soul reservoir. Many haven't mastered this exercise, still using guilt to serve their personal or professional agenda, because their emotional reservoir is filled with guilt as well.

For a child, it is hard to stand up for yourself when someone is a master at using guilt on you. Once someone sees how guilt can net them the outcome they desire, they will continue to use guilt as a mode of survival, and the tool becomes easier, more comfortable, a part of their everyday existence. Isn't the emotion of happiness or honor a better feeling to store than guilt? Of course! You can replace every single emotion you host in your reservoir.

Have you ever heard the saying, "They did the best they could" when referencing parenting skills? It's easier to say they didn't know any better than to admit that changing the pattern of negative emotion deluge onto an innocent child would have been better for all involved. If it works, and isn't broken, why fix it? (But often, it IS broke!) Parents have an enormous duty to be an emotionally healthy human prior to making a baby, which can happen without trying or planning. Rearing a child is a long job, and the bond is lasts long beyond the 18 years it takes to do it. Children learn the most about how to function from their parents and their family emotionally, mentally, physically, and spiritually. Studies show that most of this happens before they enter the school system at the age of five or six.

We, as unsuspecting novices to the Hologram of the Soul, process and believe that how we feel is our own doing and not that of someone we may love or respect. Not everyone that decides to parent or teach does so from a place of sound mental health and emotional intelligence. Sure, it starts out with wanting to give a new life every single aspect of love, nurturing, and stability as possible, but not all parents are emotionally ready to nurture their offspring in the most loving and truthful way. I've coached many people that either openly admitted they were not a good parent or were a child of a situation that didn't benefit them in the least way. How often have you heard an exhausted parent say, "You have a roof over your head, don't you?" A roof over our head doesn't necessarily nurture or prepare us for adulthood, high self-worth, and sound decision-making. A roof is a roof, and nothing more.

I suspect that less than 10% of people who choose to be parents have prepped their emotional reservoir so they can impact their offspring in a positive way. When is someone ready to make the emotional lives of others more amazing and fulfilled? The answer is and should be only after they have mastered their own emotional health and well-being.

Watch the way people hurt and shame each other. You can see it everywhere around you. It amazes me that you need a work permit to work at age 14, a license to drive, a license to get married, and yet no education to prep you for parenting—raising and nurturing children. It's a free-range opportunity of hit-and-miss, just combining cells to make a child under the guise that you host solid and effective parenting skills. That couldn't be further from the truth. Those of us who become parents, whether by natural birth, adoption, or entering via a blended family, must work on own lives and emotional reservoirs first.

Life is a hard undertaking for anyone *without* children. Now, add children to the mix! The expectation for any child should be a safe, loving, nurturing, and healthy set of parents and environment in which to absorb and learn. If you are a parent, or someone wanting to be a parent, have you ever really worked on your emotional reservoir and mental state, so you can offer your child a positive and fulfilling childhood experience? In your quiet private time, have you asked yourself, "Am I deflecting my inefficiencies onto my child? If I am, would talking to someone about my behaviors, feelings, and actions be helpful to myself and my children?" Sadly, *so few* ever explore those questions, and even fewer act on them.

We know what happens then. The cycle continues to disrupt the transference of positive feelings and emotions to those around us. We all deserve to leave the nest, familial, friendships or educational experiences *liking ourselves* and who we are as people, armed with the ability to make sound decisions on our behalf.

A child absorbs the negativity, guilt, and abuse surrounding their impressionable souls, mind; no one deserves that before they know how to handle it. Think of children who have been sexually abused. Their lives should never be impacted by something so awful.

Happily, there is an alternative. Just as a child absorbs *unhealthy*, a child can absorb *healthy*. People—parents and nonparents—are not perfect, and many people that you expose your children to won't be healthy. Personal belief systems come from somewhere outside of kids. No one is *born with them!* They are inherited. If you choose to become a parent, create a healthy environment for that child, making sure you are providing the nurture and love that, perhaps, you never received yourself.

Returning to feelings of guilt that we absorb and carry through life, those feelings come from a place of shame and of "less-than." You are not born with them, they a upon you by someone who is feeling "less than" or unworthy, themselves. Guilt may arise from religious beliefs, friends, teachers, family, parents, or other sources, but it is a psychological activity that we undertake because we picked it up along the way.

Humanity is comprised of greatness, exemplification, predators, manipulators, educated, uneducated, fully aware, and the oblivious. We must be ready to hold ourselves accountable for what we take as truth AND what we spew out as truth. We are responsible for what we allow to fill up the emotional stream of life with from our own perceptions and must be wise and watchful of our own thoughts, words and actions to positively affect others in the long-term. Learn about your emotional health first before you get into a relationship or have children. Don't be afraid to question your personal belief system and ask yourself, "What do I want to base my personal beliefs on; which values should I live my life by?"

Ultimately, how you feel about yourself depends on your dedication to sorting through your life, which may not be easy. You may have to weed through addiction, depression, anxiety, compulsion, and a lot of fears before you realize that none of this garbage that you carry around has anything to do with you. You picked it up along the way from a multitude of streams of incoming messaging. Once you embrace that concept, you'll begin to smile more and live a calmer, more peaceful life. You will be able to ask yourself if guilt, or any deep-seated negativity, belongs to you, or someone else.

I've compiled a list of words that you may feel, have felt, or have heard and absorbed along the way. The first is a compilation of positive words that generate good feelings; the other is a compilation of positive negative words that generate bad feelings. Circle the words on both lists that you felt as a child and may still feel today. As you work through these lists, it's okay to feel emotional; that's exactly what I want to happen. If it gets too overwhelming, stop and pick it up later. Some plow through the lists, while others struggle with finding a deep, personal understanding of themselves.

After you circle the words—and this may be the difficult part—ask yourself, "Where did I pick up this feeling that now thrives in my soul reservoir?" And, voila, like magic, you will see, and more importantly FEEL, where your belief system has its tentacle-hold within your soul reservoir, and how that feeling is hijacking your emotional guidance system.

This exercise starts a spiritual journey into the realms of self-esteem, your beliefs, and your outlook on life. Many learn to enjoy this journey of self-discovery. Don't be afraid to learn all the reasons why you believe the way you do about yourself and the world. We must dig deep, cleansing our souls so we may emanate healthy, happy, positive energy, emotions, and words.

I couldn't afford an expensive college education, but I've used my understanding of human psychology to help me in the business world. I am an empath; a super-student of human behavior and how healthy and unhealthy soul reservoirs affect our decision-making. We are all shiny and pretty on the outside, but on the inside, we are a compilation of feelings, chemistry, thoughts, words, and deductions that we picked up along the way.

Each word you circle, below, will give you a vivid picture of where your emotions came from.

Circle the positive emotions, feelings and thoughts that you experienced from 0-18 years of age.

Able, Absolved, Abundant, Acceptable, Accepted, Accepting, Accomplished, Accountable, Achieving, Active, Adaptable, Adequate, Admirable, Admired, Adored, Affluent, Agreeable, Alert, Ambitious, Amused, Appreciative, Appreciated, Approved, Approving, Assertive, Assured, At Ease, Attached, Attentive, Attractive, Authentic, Awake, Aware, Awesome, Balanced, Beautiful, Believing, Blessed, Blissful, Bonded, Brave, Bright, Brilliant, Calm, Capable, Captivated, Cared For, Carefree, Careful, Caring, Cautious, Centered, Certain, Cheerful, Cherished, Clean, Clear, Collected, Comfortable, Comforted, Committed, Compassionate, Complete, Composed, Comprehensive, Confident, Congruent, Connected, Conscious, Constant, Content, Cooperative, Courageous, Credible, Daring, Decisive, Defended, Delighted, Dependable, Desirable, Dignified, Discerning, Disciplined, Distinguished, Dutiful, Dynamic, Eager, Easy Going, Ecstatic, Edified, Efficient, Elated, Elegant, Elevated, Emancipated, Empowered, Encouraged, Energetic, Energized, Enthusiastic, Euphoric, Exceptional, Excited, Exhilarated, Expressive, Exuberant, Faithful, Fantastic, Favored, Firm, Flexible, Flowing, Focused, Forceful, Forgiven, Fortified, Fortunate, Free, Friendly, Fulfilled, Gentle, Genuine, Gifted,

Glowing, Good, Graceful, Gracious, Gratified, Grounded, Glowing, Guarded, Happy, Harmonious, Healed, Helpful, Heroic, High, Honest, Honorable, Honored, Hopeful, Humble, Humorous, Important, In Control, Included, Independent, Infatuated, Influential, Innocent, Inspired, Intelligent, Interested, Invigorated, Invincible, Invited, Jovial, Joyful, Jubilant, Judicious, Kind, earning, Liberated, light, Lighthearted, Loose, Loved, Loyal, Lucky, Magnetic, Marvelous, Masterful Mature, Meek, Merciful, Methodical, Mindful, Modest, Motivated, Neat, Noble, Observant, Open, Open Hearted, Organized, Pacified, Pampered, Pardoned, Passionate, Patient, Peaceful, Perfect, Persevering, Pleasant, Pleased, Popular, Positive, Powerful, Praised, Precious, Prepared, Present, Productive, Proficient, Progressive, Prosperous, protected, Prudent, Punctual, Purified, Purposeful, Qualified, Quick, Quiet, Radiant, Rational, Reasonable, Reassured, Receptive, Recognized, Redeemed, Regenerated, Relaxed, Reliable, Relieved, Remembered, Replenished, Resolute, Respected, Respectful, Responsive, Restored, Revitalized, Rewarded, Rooted, Satisfied, Secure, Selfless, Self-Reliant, Sensational, Sensible, Sensitive, Serene, Settled, Sharing, simple, Skillful, Smooth, Soothed, Spirited, Splendid, Stable, Steadfast, Strengthened, Strong, Successful, Supported, Sustained, Tactful,

Teachable, Temperate, Tender, Thankful, Thoughtful, Thrilled, Tolerant, Tranquil, Triumphant, Trusting, Understanding, Understood, Undisturbed, Unhurried, Unique, United, Unselfish, Upheld, Valiant, Valuable, Valued, Virile, Vital, Warm, Wealthy, Willing, Wise, Wonderful, Worthwhile, Worthy, Yielding, and Zealous.

Are there more? Yes, I am sure there are more, but these words should cover most of the feelings you had growing up. I suspect there is a word, or many, that already applies to that emotion, feeling or thought. As you circle the words, you'll notice why your soul reservoir and your personal happiness wanes due to an unprecedented amount of input in one direction or another. You may have equal amounts in negative and positive. It's important to now address each word/emotion/feeling to purify your soul reservoir. It doesn't take long…once you know why, you are on your way home!

Circle the negative emotions, feelings, and thoughts that you experienced from 0-18 years of age:

Abandoned, Abused, Accused, Adrift, Afraid, Aggravated, Aggressive, Agitated, Angry, Alarmed, Alienated, Alone, Aloof, Ambivalent, Anguished, Animosity, Annoyed, Antagonistic, Anxious, Apathetic, Apprehensive, Argumentative, Arrogant, Ashamed, At Fault, Attached, Avoiding, Awful, Awkward, Bad, Baffled, Banished, Barren, Bashful, Beaten Down, Befuddled, Belittled, Belligerent, Bereft, Betrayed, Bewildered, Bitter, Blaming, Bleak, Blocked, Blue, Boastful, Bored, Brokenhearted, Bugged, Burdened, Burned Up, Captive, Careless, Cast Off, Censured, Chagrined, Chaotic, Chastened, Cheap, Cheapened, Cheapened. Cheated, Childish, Clingy, Clumsy, Competitive, Compromised, Compulsive, Conceited, Condensed, confined, Conflicted, Confounded, Confused, Contemptible, Contemptuous, Contradictory, Contrary, Controlled, Covetous, Cowardly, Cranky, Crazy, Crippled, Critical, Criticized, Cruel Crushed, Cursed, Cut Off, Cynical, Debased, Deceitful, Deceived, Defamed, Defeated Defensive, Defiant, Deficient, Defiled, Deflated, Degenerate, Degraded, Dehumanized, Dejected, Demanding, Demeaned, Demoralized, Dependent, Depraved, Depreciated, Depressed, Deprived, Derided, Desecrated, Deserted, Desolate, Despair

Desperate, Destitute, Destroyed, Devalued, Devastated, Difficult, Dirty, Disappointed, Discarded Disconcerted, Discouraged, Discredited, Disgraced, Disgusted, Dismal, Dismayed, Disorganized, Disparaged, Dissatisfied, Distant, Distorted, Distressed, Distrustful, Disturbed, Dominated, Doomed, Doubtful, Down, Downcast, Drained, Dread, Dreary, Embarrassed, Embroiled, Empty, Enraged, Envious, Estranged, Exasperated, Excluded, Exhausted, Exploited, Exposed, Failure, Faithless, Fatigued, Fearful, Feeble, Filthy, Finished, Flighty, Flustered, Foggy, Forgetful, Forgotten, Forlorn, Forsaken Fragmented, Frantic, Fretful, Friendless, Frightened, Frigid, Frustrated, Fuming, Furious, Gloomy, Grieved, Grim, Grouchy, Guilty, Gullible, Harassed, Hardened, Harsh, Hasty, Hatred, Haughty, Haunted, Heartless, Helpless, Hesitant, Hindered, Hopeless, Horrible, Horrified, Hostile, Humiliated, Hurried, Hurt, Hypocritical, Hysterical, Ignorant, Immature, Immobilized,, Impaired, Impatient, Impotent, Impoverished, Imprisoned, Impulsive, In a Bind, Inadequate, Incapable, Incensed, Incompetent, Inconsiderate, Inconsistent, Indecisive, Indignant, Ineffective, Inefficient, Inept, Inferior, Inflexible, Infuriated, Inhibited, Insecure, Insignificant, Insincere, Insulted Intimidated, Irresponsible, Irritable, Isolated, Jealous, Jittery, Joyless, Judgmental, Jumpy, Lacking, Left

Out, Let Down, Limited, Listless, Livid, Lonely, Lonesome, Longing, Lost, Lousy, Low ,Mad, Malicious, Maligned, Manipulated, Materialistic, Mean, Melancholy, Minimized, Miserable, Miserly, Mistreated, Misunderstood, Misused, Mixed Up, Mocked, Moody, Mortified, Mournful, Muddled, Naïve, Narrow, Nauseated, Negative, Neglected, Nervous, Obnoxious, Obsessed, Obstinate, Obstructed, Offended, On Edge, Opinioned, Opposed, Opposition Oppressed, Outcast, Outraged, Overlooked, Overwhelmed, Overworked, Pained, Panicky, Parlayed, Paranoid, Peculiar, Perfectionistic, Perplexed, Persecuted, Perturbed Pessimistic, Phobic, Phony, Pitiful, Powerless, Prejudiced, Pressured, Punished, puny, Pushed, Put Down, puzzled, Rattled, Rebellious, Regretful, Rejected, Remorseful, Remote, Reproved, Repulsive, Resentful, Resistant, Responsible, Restless, Restrained, Restricted, Ridiculed, Risky, Rotten, Ruined, Rushed, Ruthless, Sad, Sarcastic, Scared, Scattered, Scoffed At, Scorned, Seething, Shaky, Shallow, Shameful, Shocked, Shot Down, Shunned, Shy, Sick, Sinful, Slammed, Slandered, Slighted, Slow, Small, Smothered, Smug, Sorrowful, Spiteful, Stagnant, Stifled, Stingy, Stressed, Stubborn, Stumped, Stupid, Suffering, Suicidal, Superficial, Superior, Suspicious, Tactless, Tearful, Temperamental, Tense, Terrible, Terrified, Thoughtless, Threatened, Thwarted,

Timid, Tired, Tortured, Trapped, Troubled, Turned Off, Unable, Unappreciated, Uncertain, Unclean, Unclear, Uncomfortable, Undecided, Undesirable, Undisciplined, Uneasy, Unforgivable, Unforgiving, Unfriendly, Unhappy, Unimportant, Unmindful, Unorganized, Unpleasant, Unprotected, Unreasonable, Unsettled, Unsure, Unthankful, Unwanted, Unwise, Unworthy, Upset, Uptight, Used, Useless, Vengeful, Vexed, Vicious, Vindictive, Violated, Violent, Vulnerable, Washed Up, Wasted, Weak, Weepy, Withdrawn, Worried, Worthless, Wounded, Wrong, Yearning

Here are additional words:

Accused, Agony, Battered, Can't Breathe, Chained, Claustrophobic, Damned, Different, Disappointed, Disgraced, Don't Belong, Don't Exist, Extrovert, Foolish, Forgotten, Freakish, Frightened, Garbage, Irresponsible, Lazy, Losing My Mind, Lustful, Mental, Not Needed, Numb, Offended, Outcast, Over Exposed, People Pleaser, Powerless, Pressured, Prideful, Put-Down, Raped, Repulsed, Ridiculed, Screwed, Seduced, Selfish, Shattered, Sickened, Small, Smothered, Stupid, Terrified, Thrown Away, Tormented, Two-Faced, Unaccepted, Unfeeling, Un-feminine, Unloved, Un-Motivated

Again, as you circle the words, you'll notice why your soul reservoir and your personal happiness wanes or is suffering due to an unprecedented amount of input in one direction or another. You may have equal amounts in negative and positive. It's important to now address each word/emotion/feeling to purify your soul reservoir.

Go through the list and count all the positive emotions and all the negative emotions that derived from your childhood experiences from every area of input. The next exercise involves determining WHY you have these feelings. What did it stem from, who delivered the positive or negative, and are the feelings / emotions warranted, justified, deserved, or legitimate? Did those feelings serve you or hinder you throughout your life? The feelings may have come from teachers, friends, clergy, family, parents, siblings and or authority figures of some sort. Maybe someone changed how you felt about yourself completely in such a positive way that they are still important to you today. Each word you circle, a very vivid picture of where its origin in your soul reservoir will become evident.

This chapter is extremely important to your personal journey to ongoing personal happiness. Once you clarify why you carry those feelings and emotions around as an adult, you'll be able to purify your reservoir and compartmentalize, or snuff out, those feelings. Once and for you, you can cleanse the soul reservoir of any trouble spots concerning confidence and self-esteem. Going through this exercise is not easy and I believe some will never tend to the soul reservoir. But this book is about wisdom for personal happiness and I believe without a doubt in efforts to be authentically happy the reservoir must be met on a personal level.

Chapter 16

Hologram of the Soul

After the cleansing process has started or is quasi completed, the feeling of overwhelming happiness and your view on life can be incredibly serene and exciting. Honestly when I relinquished the hold my negative soul environment had on me, feeling happy felt a little unnerving. I hadn't spent much time in a happy state of being. Feeling freedom and happiness from a cleansed soul reservoir, and a new bright, weightless hologram, can make us feel extremely vulnerable. We have become a different person on a new journey to stay true to self. After I did all the cleansing of my soul reservoir, I felt the vulnerability and responsibility to stay in a happy state. How could I handle something so awesome when all my years of training were in the state of disarray, bewilderment, questioning and unhappiness?

Being uncomfortable with your new state of being is synonymous with the beginnings of a new relationship. Trusting your new way of feeling and decision making is the outstanding overall variable. We will embark on a new *self-love* relationship with a whole new set of parameters. To those of us that have not felt or maintained a pure, serene, and self-relinquishing happiness state of being—because we haven't felt any real happiness for a long time—the emotions after soul-cleansing may feel oddly foreign and uncomfortable. In times of true happiness, we are in congruency with what <u>we</u> know to be true, who <u>we are</u>, and in alignment with what <u>we want</u> and in our soul. The soul is the foundational navigational system that narrates your lifelong happiness. Work on the continuation of guarding emotional dispatch and cleansing the soul reservoir and life will be good!

For much of my life, being in a state of calmness and joy wasn't my norm. I wasn't sure how to get to a state of happiness, so, I embarked on the journey of "soul cleansing." I said, what is the feeling I am feeling, why do I have that feeling, where did it come from and why am I holding in so close to my soul and why does it direct my output? I just knew I wasn't ME inside this body and I needed to shake off what wasn't me in efforts to be me! When we are accustomed to suppressing happiness to align with what is most comfortable in our soul reservoir, we live, quite blindly, in a state of discomfort. We inherited our soul reservoir, so we align with what we know. But when you know you are more than what you inherited you become to take shape into who you want to be! We grow accustomed to those less-than-happy feelings, so things *must be okay.* But it's not okay, especially if we didn't put those feelings in our soul reservoir in the first place.

Some people will, and in a very bold fashion, seek forms of pleasure because their goal is to not feel the pains of what was inherited. Denial is a happy place for many but befriending and supporting denial can destroy a life. Denial can work temporarily, but ultimately the results are less than ideal. Most humans aren't wired to feel happiness 24/7. Even after all these years of cleansing my soul reservoir, I know there will be days ahead of me where I will struggle with unsuspecting emotions whether self-delivered or ill-gotten gain from someone or somewhere else. It's likely I won't be able to immediately explain what has made a home inside my soul but there will always be some work to do.

Remember, emotions form our guidance system for life. Understanding them, their origins, and the need to hold or dispel them is essential to a happy life. When you understand which emotions are making their way into your reservoir and onto to your hologram, life begins to take shape in the form of happiness. The slightest change in our soul chemistry—from entrance of, or recurrence of a thought pattern—can alter the hologram for minutes or days at a time. A healthy, fully disclosed and cleansed soul reservoir is the only way to live a pure, content, and complete life of happiness.

Achieving and maintaining a radiant hologram of the soul takes work. When you jump ahead and skip the work that is needed, then where you go, so goes the polluted reservoir and hologram. The sooner you can dip your proverbial toe in the water of inherited negative emotions and begin the course of cleansing your soul reservoir, the sooner you'll reach greater heights of true personal happiness. Start by asking the hard questions. Attack all the negative emotions you carry and learn the origin of each emotion and host it or annihilate it.

Hologram of the Soul isn't about blaming the generations before, or the 4th grade teacher of the kids that made horrible fun of you for being different. It's about accepting your place card today in life of your own emotional state. Taking accountability for why you feel the way you do no matter how it made a home in your soul. Knowing an uncomfortable chemistry lingers floating in your reservoir is why you start the process at all. You know you wake up with it each day, do something about it. I was born with an insatiable desire for life, people and myself. I felt the energy and chemistry within my own soul at such a young age that it was evident to me and everyone around me this baby, this child is really someone incredibly gifted and a shining star. The love I had inside of me couldn't be contained within the walls of my humanness, heart, or soul. I was an enigma and no matter where I went everyone was drawn to me. How many young children can completely love themselves at such an early age? I did. But as I emerged into a familiar system, social system, educational system I absorbed emotional chemistry from everyone around me, and all the environments. I knew at an early age I was becoming a different person and I started taking in feelings that led to an unwanted and unauthorized journey of aligning with emotional unhappiness versus true happiness. My hologram changed in the 3rd grade drastically. Years leading up to that time, something was changing me. You could visibly see it and I felt it. It wasn't okay to have "feelings" or "emotions" and it was never okay to openly express them. Emotional intelligence wasn't an accepted topic until recently. But I've been emotionally intelligent since as far back as I can remember. I wanted to address every emotion I had, and it didn't bother me at all to talk about them. Just the fact I knew what I was feeling was enough of a deterrent to not address me. I am a FIRM believer you must feel all emotions to feel alive and present in life! I encourage all my clients to feel present and alive versus operating on auto pilot and denial.

As an adult, finding the core to my third-grade hologram was my initial emotional work. The work would be to figure out who I became before I knew who I was. My reservoir filled up with emotions that were not my own and until 2008, I didn't dive into my soul reservoir to understand exactly why I felt the way I did. So, in efforts to never blame anyone, I dealt with the emotions I was feeling to change who I had become. The journey of self-discovery is not without tears or acceptance. The journey is awesomely freeing.

In the beginning of my life, early on, I was a happy kid... and now after handling all the work to abolish negative soul chemistry and self-deprivation, I'm finally back at that place I want to be, *a happy kid!* Don't let anyone steal your hologram. Not today and not ever! Thank you.

Made in the USA
Monee, IL
01 September 2020